This book is a powerful honesty, faith, and hope, Merrily courageously shares her miraculous journey from a diagnosis of cancer to complete healing. Many others share their insights. Every page overflows with the reality of God's presence, the power of prayer, and the unwavering truth that nothing is impossible for Him. This is not just theoretical teaching, but it is filled with stories of divine intervention, deep faith, and the kind of hope that breathes life into hearts. Whether you're personally in need of healing or standing in the gap for someone who is, this book will strengthen your faith and stir your spirit. A must-read for anyone believing for healing!

DR WALT LANDERS, SENIOR PASTOR
THE LIFE CHURCH (TLC) FOUNDER AND CHANCELLOR/CEO OF
TEXAS LEADERSHIP PUBLIC SCHOOLS
SAN ANGELO, TEXAS, USA

If you have ever desired to pray for the sick but didn't know where to start, this is your handbook. Rev. Merrily Madero, a woman of deep faith, has created an incredibly clear and actionable guide. It's more than a book; it's a vital tool to empower every Christian to do the work of the ministry.

REV. SABRINA CHOW, SENIOR PASTOR
RISEN CHRISTIAN ASSEMBLY
SINGAPORE

The *Biblical Healing Handbook* by Merrily Madero is a faith-filled, power packed resource that brings clarity and confidence to believers seeking God's healing power. She engages some of the most probing questions today concerning, why do some get healed and others do not? With both the precision of a seasoned leader from her years as a Colonel in the U.S. Air Force, and the compassion of a servant of Christ, Merrily answers these pressing questions on divine healing with biblical truth and grace. Every page inspires faith, restores hope, and reminds us that Jesus still heals today.

APOSTLE LES BOWLING, SENIOR PASTOR
EAGLEROCK CHURCH AND EAGLEROCK COVENANT NETWORK
COLUMBUS, OHIO, USA

I have always been a big fan of ministry books that are very grounded and have immediate application. Merrily Madero does this well in regard to the ministry of healing. This is a great book for any believer asking practical questions about this important ministry.

JARED DIETRICH, MISSIONARY
ASSEMBLIES OF GOD MISSIONARY TO MONGOLIA
ULAANBAATAR, MONGOLIA

What I love most about the *Biblical Healing Handbook* is how it flows out of Merrily's heart and passion for this subject. It doesn't just teach about healing—it helps you feel God's desire to bring hope, restoration, and wholeness. This book will encourage your faith and give you practical steps to minister healing with confidence and compassion. This resource equips leaders and believers alike with biblical insight, pastoral wisdom, and real-world application. It is a timely and much-needed guide for the church today.

JIM WESTHEIM, EXECUTIVE PASTOR
FAITH ALIVE CHURCH
WEST BRANCH, MICHIGAN, USA

Our main responsibility in front of illnesses and diseases is to strongly believe the word of God and boldly proclaim it. God will always remain faithful to answer our prayers according to what the precious sacrifice of His Son Jesus Christ did on the Calvary's cross. This *Biblical Healing Handbook* is a clear, Scripture-based guide that equips the church to minister healing with confidence and compassion. Merrily points out by the precious power of the Holy Spirit, healing spirit is still available no matter what challenges we may faced with. Right now, dear readers, receive healing for free, and remain healed. Amen!

REV KOKORA JEAN DIDIER BÉDO, SENIOR PASTOR
EVANGEL PENTECOSTAL CHURCH, QUÉBEC, CANADA
CÔTE D'IVOIRE, AFRICA, ASSEMBLIES OF GOD CHURCH
MISSIONARY IN CANADA
CERTIFIED COACH OF PENTECOSTAL ASSEMBLIES OF CANADA,
DISTRICT OF QUÉBEC

Jesus spent much of His time on Earth bringing God's healing mercy to the sick, afflicted, troubled, possessed and forgiving sinners. In all our sufferings as we seek the healing hand of Jesus, He invites us to join our suffering with Him on the cross and to receive then His care and compassion. My dear friend and servant of the Lord, Merrily Madero, in her inspiring and wisdom filled book—*Biblical Healing Handbook: 25 of Your Healing Questions Answered*, shares many prayerful spiritual, pastoral and good loving human ways we can open our hearts and lives to the healing presence of the Holy Spirit today.

BISHOP MICHAEL D. PFEIFER, OMI, D.D.
BISHOP EMERITUS OF THE CATHOLIC DIOCESE OF SAN ANGELO
SAN ANTONIO, TEXAS, USA

The *Biblical Healing Handbook* is a timely and faith-filled resource for the church. It provides clear, Scripture-based answers to questions believers have about healing. This book will strengthen faith, encourage prayer, and point people to Jesus, our true Healer.

HIBROON KHOKHAR, PASTOR AND EVANGELIST
UNIVERSAL GOSPEL ASSEMBLY CHURCH OF PAKISTAN
KARACHI, PAKISTAN

Merrily has written a well-researched and excellent healing handbook that warrants all believers to have in their library. It addresses the glories and mysteries of biblical healing.

APOSTLE, DR. LANA HEIGHTLEY, FOUNDER AND PRESIDENT
WOMEN WITH A MISSION
PARKER, COLORADO, USA

This book is a very handy helpful biblical informative framework to equip us how to minister to the sick. I also appreciate the valuable insights and testimonies of the different ministry leaders.

LISA CHIN, PASTOR
REVIVAL CENTRE ASSEMBLY OF GOD CHURCH
KUALA LUMPUR, MALAYSIA

If you believe that healing is for today and that anyone can be used by the Lord to bring healing to anyone, this book is for you. The biblical foundations and actual experiences mentioned in this book will give you the confidence and competence to minister healing to anyone.

JILL BOYONAS, ASIA AND PHILIPPINES
DIRECTOR CHURCH MULTIPLICATION COALITION INTERNATIONAL
PHILIPPINES

Merrily has put all of her heart and gift of teaching into this practical guide to answer all of our questions about healing. By drawing from the Word of God and respected ministers around the world, she has compiled a helpful resource for anyone seeking to understand and walk in God's healing power.

MARY, MISSIONARY TO ASIA

As a seasoned minister, preacher and teacher of the Word of God, Reverend Merrily gives a complete overview towards the ministry of healing. In a day and age where the ministry of healing is very much misused and misunderstood, I believe this *Biblical Healing Handbook* by Reverend Merrily will truly shed light and give a complete, purposeful and experiential view of what it means to do and to receive the divine healing of our God the ultimate Healer. I'm certain without any doubts that this handbook will be an immense blessing and resource to every leader and believer.

DAVID PAUL, SENIOR PASTOR
SMYRNA CHURCH,
NUWARA ELIYA, SRI LANKA

Must read for the body of Christ on the subject of wholesome healing. Reverend Merrily, with her best, not only equips us with the profound knowledge of healing but also ministers us to be healed from various kinds of diseases in her *Biblical Healing Handbook*. This book is needed in every believer's home to fight against the challenges of sickness and enjoy God's miracles in everyday life.

WASEEM YOUSAF, SENIOR PASTOR AND FOUNDER
HARVEST CHURCH MINISTRIES OF PAKISTAN
LAHORE, PAKISTAN

BIBLICAL HEALING HANDBOOK

25 OF *YOUR* HEALING QUESTIONS ANSWERED

Merrily Madero

Merrily Madero Ministries International

Biblical Healing Handbook
© 2025 Merrily Madero

All rights reserved. No part of this publication may be reproduced in any form without written permission from the author.

Unless otherwise indicated, all Scripture references are from THE HOLY BIBLE, NEW INTERNATIONAL VERSION®, NIV® Copyright © 1973, 1978, 1984, 2011 by Biblica, Inc.® Used by permission. All rights reserved worldwide. Other versions used include: ESV® Bible (The Holy Bible, English Standard Version®), © 2001 by Crossway, a publishing ministry of Good News Publishers. ESV Text Edition: 2025. The ESV text may not be quoted in any publication made available to the public by a Creative Commons license. The ESV may not be translated in whole or in part into any other language. Used by permission. All rights reserved; New King James Version®. Copyright © 1982 by Thomas Nelson. Used by permission. All rights reserved; the *Holy Bible*, New Living Translation, copyright © 1996, 2004, 2015 by Tyndale House Foundation. Used by permission of Tyndale House Publishers, Inc., Carol Stream, Illinois 60188. All rights reserved; the New Century Version®. Copyright © 2005 by Thomas Nelson. Used by permission. All rights reserved; and the King James Version. New American Bible (Revised Edition) (NABRE). Scripture texts, prefaces, introductions, footnotes and cross references used in this work are taken from the New American Bible, revised edition © 2010, 1991, 1986, 1970 Confraternity of Christian Doctrine, Inc., Washington, DC All Rights Reserved. No part of this work may be reproduced or transmitted in any form or by any means, electronic or mechanical, including photocopying, recording, or by any information storage and retrieval system, without permission in writing from the copyright owner.

ISBN-13: 979-8-9937219-0-3

Cover Concept Design by Bélynda Casse
Shutterstock Cover Image AI Creation

Printed in the United States of America
1 2 3 4 5 6 7 8 9 10 Printing/Year 29 28 27 26 25

This book is dedicated to my husband, Joël Casse.

*Only the Lord could have brought us together
in such a divine manner.
You are exactly what I needed as a helpmate and
ministry partner.
It was worth the twelve-year wait for the Lord to bring you,
my perfect partner in life.*

*I appreciate all the "extra" things you did as I was stuck
at my computer writing this book, as well as your endless
support for my ministry and crazy travel schedule.*

*I cherish every minute with you and especially the times we
get to serve the Lord together.*

Thank you, Husband!

Acknowledgments	11
List of Ministry Leaders Interviewed	13
Foreword by Superintendent Aaron Hlavin, Assemblies of God Michigan Ministry Network	15
Introduction	17
Part I: What Should I Know About Biblical Healing?	21
Chapter 1: Is Healing Still Happening Today?	23
Chapter 2: If God Loves Us, Why Is There Sickness?	29
Chapter 3: Who Actually Does the Healing?	39
Chapter 4: Can Anyone Pray for Healing?	43
Chapter 5: What Is the Most Important Thing Needed for Healing?	49
Chapter 6: Are There Different Ways to Bring Healing?	55
Chapter 7: How Were People Healed in the Bible?	61
Chapter 8: Can We Receive Healing for Our Spirit?	67
Chapter 9: Can We Receive Soul Healing (Which Includes Emotional Healing)?	73
Chapter 10: How Are Our Bodies Healed Today?	83
Part II: What Are the Answers to Difficult Healing Questions?	89
Chapter 11: Why Isn't Everyone Healed?	91
Chapter 12: Can People Lose Their Healing?	103
Chapter 13: Is There Healing from a Harmful Lifestyle?	109
Chapter 14: Does God Heal Old-Age Ailments?	119
Chapter 15: How Should We Navigate End-of-Life Situations?	125
Chapter 16: Are People Still Raised from the Dead Today?	133
Chapter 17. How Does Demon Deliverance Factor into Healing?	139

Part III: What About Me? What Should I Do? 149

Chapter 18: How Do I Prepare? 151

Chapter 19: Where and When Should I Pray for Healing? 163

Chapter 20: Is There a Checklist of What I Should Say and Do? 169

Chapter 21: Is There a Checklist of What I Should Not Say and Do? 173

Part IV: Is There Good Advice as I Begin This Journey of Praying for Others? 175

Chapter 22: What Mistakes Do Believers Make When Praying for Healing? 177

Chapter 23: What Is the Best Advice and Encouragement from Each Ministry Leader? 185

Chapter 24: What Are Some Real Healing Stories? 195

Chapter 25: What Are Some Sample Healing Prayers? 207

Appendix: Steps to Become a Believer and Lead Others to Jesus 211

Notes 215

About the Author 217

ACKNOWLEDGMENTS

First and foremost, I give glory to my Father God, through my Savior Jesus Christ, and thank Him for the privilege to write this Holy Spirit–inspired book for Him and His church.

Next, a big thank you to my daughter, Dr. Leia Fecteau, MD, who was my main editor as I put this book together. Just like in my last book, she was instrumental in organizing, editing, and reminding me of key biblical verses I failed to include. She also provided a "doctor's perspective" to this healing book. I appreciate her long hours of effort, during her precious little free time while serving as the chief resident for a challenging five-year Internal Medicine and Emergency Medicine Residency Program, and applaud her follow-on fellowship in Critical Care at Long Island Jewish Medical Center in New York.

Also, a sincere thank you to the twenty ministry leaders I interviewed for this book. Their words added significantly to what the Lord wants His church to know about how to pray for healing in others. I'm blessed to have worked with each one of them over the years and look forward to working together again for the kingdom of God here on this earth.

I truly appreciate the comments, support, and friendship provided by Licensed Professional Counselor Brenda Rogers. Her expertise provided excellent guidance and the right words concerning spiritual and emotional healing.

A special thanks to Pam Holifield, my dear friend of over forty years, who reviewed every page for corrections. Additional thanks to her, along with Phil White and Lana Heightley, who serve on the board of directors for my ministry, Merrily Madero Ministries, M3 International, which we will refer to as M3 International.

Thanks to my publisher, Karen Pickering and her staff at KMP Publishing Services.

Most of all, a gigantic thank you to the faithful friends, churches, and supporters of M3 International, whose prayers and financial support made publishing this book possible.

LIST OF MINISTRY LEADERS INTERVIEWED

1. AD, John, Senior Pastor and Founder, Consuming Fire Ministries and Kings TV, Lahore, Pakistan
2. Bowling, Les, Apostle, Senior Pastor, Eagle Rock Church Network, Columbus, OH, USA
3. Boyonas, Jill, Asia and Philippines Director, Church Multiplication Coalition International, based out of the Philippines
4. Chin, Lisa, Pastor, Revival Center, Assemblies of God Church, Kuala Lumpur, Malaysia
5. Chow, Sabrina, Senior Pastor, Risen Christian Assembly, Singapore
6. Dietrich, Jared, Missionary to Mongolia, Assemblies of God, Ulaanbataatar, Mongolia
7. Dowdy, Naomi, Apostle, Assemblies of God Former Senior Pastor and Mentor, Singapore
8. Gill, Tanveer, Evangelist, Al Ain, United Arab Emirates (UAE)
9. Heightley, Lana, Apostle, Dr (D.Min), Reverend, President and Founder of Women with a Mission (WWAM), Parker, CO, USA
10. Hlavin, Aaron, Network Superintendent, Assemblies of God Michigan Ministry Network, Brighton, Michigan, USA
11. Khokhar, Hibroon, Pastor and Evangelist, Universal Gospel Assembly Church of Pakistan, Karachi, Pakistan
12. Kokora, Didier, Senior Pastor, Evangel Pentecostal, Québec City, Québec, Canada, and Assemblies of God Missionary to Canada from Côte d'Ivoire, Africa
13. Landers, Walt, Senior Pastor, Dr (PhD), The Life Church (TLC), Founder and Chancellor/CEO of Texas Leadership Public Schools, San Angelo, TX, USA
14. Lemons, Powell, Retired Pastor, Evangelist, Fresno, CA, USA (*now deceased*)

15. Missionary Mary, based out of the Philippines, but Worldwide Missions Work
16. Paul, David, Senior Pastor, Smyrna Church, Nuwara Eliya, Sri Lanka
17. Pfeifer, Michael, Catholic Bishop, OMI, D.D., *Bishop Emeritus of the Diocese of San Angelo*, San Antonio, TX, USA
18. Westheim, Jim, Executive Pastor, Faith Alive Church, West Branch, MI, USA
19. Worldwide Evangelist, Mr., based out USA, but Worldwide Missions Work
20. Yousaf, Waseem, Pastor and Founder, Harvest Church Ministries of Pakistan, Lahore, Pakistan

FOREWORD

I believe in healing! I firmly believe that God is a God of healing. Personally, I believe that God still heals today! I have experienced several healings in my life, including one time when God healed a severe burn from hot water—blisters disappeared, and no scars were left. I've also experienced the remarkable healing of my knees during a service.

I also understand the struggles of needing healing and not yet receiving it. Since 1999, I've lived with a muscle disorder that causes pain, soreness, and discomfort almost daily. Still, I have never stopped—nor will I ever stop—believing in the healing power of my Savior. Healing isn't always quick, nor does it always happen as we expect, but it's always within God's reach.

Throughout the Bible, we see that Jesus heals every disease and sickness.

> Jesus went throughout Galilee, teaching in their synagogues, proclaiming the good news of the kingdom, and healing every disease and sickness among the people. News about him spread all over Syria, and people brought to him all who were ill with various diseases, those suffering severe pain, the demon-possessed, those having seizures, and the paralyzed; and he healed them. (Matthew 4:23-24, NIV)

The truth is that He has no limits. He heals the body, the soul, and the spirit. Yet, this very subject has been a source of confusion and division within the Christian community. We rarely question whether God can heal, but we often wrestle with questions about how healing occurs, why it sometimes doesn't happen, and how we should respond when prayers go unanswered.

As a minister, I have prayed and witnessed God perform miracles that left me speechless with awe. But I have also borne the burden of disappointment when healing didn't happen as I had hoped. These struggles test our faith, but they also deepen our understanding of God's sovereignty and His heart for His people.

That is why this book is so essential.

In the *Biblical Healing Handbook*, Merrily Madero draws on decades of ministry, personal experience, and her own miraculous healing—her recovery from pancreatic cancer in 2008—to address one of the most pressing and misunderstood areas of the Christian life. With biblical clarity and practical wisdom, she lays a foundation for understanding how God heals today, why sickness exists, and how believers can pray with both faith and humility.

Across its four parts, this book equips readers to think, believe, and pray more deeply about healing. This is not a book of formulas or "quick fixes." Healing cannot be reduced to the right words, the correct method, or the right person. It is always a sovereign act of God. As Merrily so beautifully explains, healing is about trusting God's heart, resting in His power, and recognizing that every healing—whether physical, emotional, or spiritual—is a gift of His grace.

Merrily is uniquely qualified to write this book. A retired U.S. Air Force Colonel with over thirty years of leadership experience, she has commanded men and women with distinction and excellence. She holds degrees in Mechanical Engineering and Theology, with advanced studies at Troy University, National Defense University, and Air Command and Staff College. She has traveled to 119 nations, ministered in twenty-four of them, and leads an international ministry dedicated to preaching, teaching, and equipping believers worldwide. Above all, she is a living testimony of God's healing power and a faithful servant who continues to proclaim the truth of Jesus Christ wherever He sends her.

This book is for those who have experienced God's healing firsthand, as well as for those who are still waiting and praying for their own miracle. My prayer is that as you read, your faith will be encouraged, your questions will be met with biblical wisdom, and your heart will be drawn closer to the Great Physician.

Read with an open Bible, an open mind, and an open heart because the same Jesus who healed in the days of Scripture is still healing today.

Aaron Hlavin, Network Superintendent
Assemblies of God Michigan Ministry Network, USA

INTRODUCTION

I was told if my surgery went well, I could live two to five more years. That was seventeen years ago now. In 2008 I was diagnosed with a golf ball–sized pancreatic tumor that through a biopsy was categorized as a malignant neoplasm, or very cancerous tumor. I was stunned as I sat in my doctor's office. This diagnosis came just seven months after my own mother's short but devastating battle with pancreatic cancer that ended in her passing in less than three months. I was concerned I would share the same fate, and I immediately spiraled into an internal battle of conflicting emotions. First, I started to feel excitement to meet Jesus in heaven and live out eternity with no more pain or sorrow, but then the next minute I would plunge into a deep grief and sadness to leave my daughter, a teenager at the time, motherless and to miss her maturing into the amazing woman she would become.

My surgeon recommended a procedure called a "Whipple," which is a complex surgery involving removal of part of the pancreas, stomach, biliary ducts, and small bowel, and reconnecting everything back together in a new way, with the goal of removing the tumor and any surrounding tissue the cancer may have invaded. Before the surgery, I was at the peak of my thirty-year career in the United States Air Force, at the rank of colonel and serving in the role of vice wing commander of the 17th Training Wing at Goodfellow Air Force Base, in San Angelo, Texas. This type of surgery is uncommon and needed to take place at Wilford Hall Medical Center in San Antonio, a specialized surgical center three hours away from my home in West Texas at the time.

Before I left, I asked my church family and Senior Pastor Walt Landers to pray over me. I had begun to feel in my spirit that the Lord was telling me, "You're not done!" and that I would be healed. I didn't fully understand at the time why or how this healing would manifest in me, but I had no doubt in my message from the Lord.

My surgery lasted nine hours, and I was in the hospital recovering for over three weeks. The first time my surgeon came in to talk to me, I remember the astonishment in his voice when he revealed the pathology results on my tumor did not show a trace of the malignancy that had been detected on my initial biopsies. Twice more my surgeon came in to tell me

I would not need chemotherapy, nor radiation, nor any additional cancer treatment. He couldn't explain how my tumor went from a very cancerous malignant tumor to a benign noncancerous tumor. I knew at that moment I had been miraculously healed by God.

I healed quickly, and as I gained back my strength over the next many months, my doctors continued to be amazed at my progress. I was told that many patients develop diabetes after the procedure from the removal of the pancreas or develop chronic malabsorption issues that can lead to critical vitamin deficiencies due to the smaller stomach and bowel. Matter of fact, I was in such good shape physically, a few years later I volunteered to deploy to Afghanistan in 2011 for over a year. To this day, I remain free from diabetes and have only minimal gastroenterological symptoms, allowing me to live a healthy and normal life, have an (almost) normal diet, and travel the world trying all the new and interesting foods I can. Praise the Lord!

So yes, I believe that God still performs miraculous healing today and have found a personal passion in praying for healing in others. However, that does not mean I have been miraculously healed of every sickness and injury in my life. It took a lot of time in prayer with the Lord to understand why I was healed of cancer, but not every other aliment throughout my life. I will share some of what the Lord told me throughout this book.

I wrote this book for those who are a part of the Lord's Church today, to help remove some of the mystery surrounding healing. Since 2016, I have traveled around the world as a preacher, teacher, and missionary, and I've seen a lot of frustration regarding who, how, and why one can pray for healing. Some have told me they don't pray for others for healing because they don't know how. Others have told me that they prayed for someone once, didn't see healing, and never tried again. I have heard believers incorrectly proclaim that only a pastor can pray for people to be healed. So many people in the Lord's Church are confused about who, when, and why we should pray for healing.

The Lord told me to write this book to provide a handbook for all believers to help take the mystery out of healing. It will answer twenty-five of your biggest questions on healing. My goal is to provide a solid biblical background on healing, including answering those difficult questions, as well as provide simple checklists on what you need to know, how to prepare, what to do and not do when you pray for others and yourself for healing.

I am blessed there have been many times the Lord has used me as His instrument to bring about miraculous healing when I have prayed for others, but this does not happen every time. I have prayed for hundreds of people over the years to receive healing, and I can remember only a small number who received immediate healing, some who I know were healed later and the rest I believe God healed in His way. This book will try to explain some of the reasons why some are immediately healed and others are not.

This book is based completely on the Bible; however, for a few of the questions in this book, there is not a definitive biblical answer. As an ordained minister with the Assemblies of God, I have experience and formal education on many topics surrounding healing and have developed my own personal practice of healing within my ministry, but I feel the topic is too broad for me to consider myself an expert in this area. So for this book I interviewed twenty other ministry leaders to get their perspectives and experiences on healing. These ministry leaders are from nine different countries and have a range of titles and backgrounds including missionaries, pastors, evangelists, and ministry directors. I did my best to provide a range of perspectives from these leaders to help you think through the questions in each chapter, even if their answers differ slightly from my own. Many held similar views; however, to avoid repetition I only included comments from one of the ministry leaders. Their comments are scattered throughout the book. In chapter 23, each ministry leader provided their own words to give you the best advice possible as you embark on this healing journey. Their complete titles, positions, and country locations are listed prior to this Introduction.

This is the book the Lord wanted me to write for YOU. It is meant to encourage you to pray for healing in others. I could have written a book on each of these chapters, and there probably are books on each of these questions if you desire further study. However, this is meant to be a reference book, with the goal of giving brief and directed answers to many of the most common questions surrounding healing. It should provide you with background knowledge about healing from the Bible and provide relevant supporting Scripture for every chapter. It will also give you detailed instruction on how, where, when, and why you can pray for others for healing.

Each chapter's title is a frequently asked question related to healing, and the main points will build throughout the chapters. I recommend reading the entire book through and then going back when needed to reference a specific point of healing.

Part I: What Should I Know About Biblical Healing? (chapters 1 through 10) will teach you what you need to know about basic biblical healing and provide a solid foundation as you start your journey praying for others.

Part II: What Are the Answers to Difficult Healing Questions? (chapters 11 through 17) will answer the most difficult questions many people have about healing, such as "Why isn't everyone healed?" and "Can people lose their healing?" In these chapters you will find a range of viewpoints from several of the ministry leaders.

Part III: What About Me? What Should I Do? (chapters 18 through 21) will provide practical guidelines and checklists to use as you prepare to pray for healing in others.

Part IV: Is There Good Advice as I Begin This Journey of Praying for Others? (chapters 22 through 25) walks you through the many mistakes people make about healing and provides you the best advice and encouragement from our ministry leaders. It also contains healing stories and sample healing prayers.

Once you read this book, you will be energized, trained, and equipped to pray for healing for yourself and for others. My prayer is this book will both educate and encourage you to go be the healer the Lord needs you to be to further his kingdom here on the earth.

Heavenly Father, let this book be an educational guide for everyone who reads it. May it educate, inform, and equip those who desire to pray for healing in others. We pray in the name of Jesus Christ, Amen.

Part I:
WHAT SHOULD I KNOW ABOUT BIBLICAL HEALING?

Chapter 1

IS HEALING STILL HAPPENING TODAY?

Yes! Healing in the name of Jesus Christ is still happening today.

What Does the Bible Say About This Question?

Psalm 107:19-20: "Then they cried to the Lord in their trouble, and he saved them from their distress. He sent out his word and healed them; he rescued them from the grave."

Isaiah 53:4-5: "Surely he took up our pain and bore our suffering, yet we considered him punished by God, stricken by him, and afflicted. But he was pierced for our transgressions, he was crushed for our iniquities; the punishment that brought us peace was on him, and by his wounds we are healed."

1 Peter 2:24: "'He himself bore our sins' in his body on the cross, so that we might die to sins and live for righteousness; 'by his wounds you have been healed.'"

James 5:14-15a: "Is anyone among you sick? Let them call the elders of the church to pray over them and anoint them with oil in the name of the Lord. And the prayer offered in faith will make the sick person well; the Lord will raise them up."

Let's Look Deeper:

I can testify that the Lord healed me miraculously from pancreatic cancer as I shared in the introduction. I have also seen healings in many friends and throughout my ministry work and travels. In addition, all twenty of the ministry leaders I interviewed believe God's Word confirms healing is for today, and all have witnessed healings from the Lord take place in their ministries. Let's look at some ministry leaders' unique perspectives on the question, "Is healing still happening today?"

> **Evangelist Tanveer Gill**: It is God's will for healing, for every time, for every place, for every situation, and for every person.

> **Pastor Hibroon Khokhar**: Healing is a gift of love that flows directly from the heart of our Father in heaven. God desires healing for the whole person–body, soul (mind, emotions, will), and spirit. We receive healing in Jesus' name through the power of the Holy Spirit. Jesus came to bring salvation and healing to the world and to destroy the devil's work.

> **Superintendent Aaron Hlavin**: God is in the healing business, not just physically but mind, soul, and spirit. God's healing evidence is all around us in so many ways. Look at Psalm 107:19-20; it's a beautiful picture of what God's Word does. It is what brings faith: faith is by hearing and hearing by the Word of God. When God's Word goes out, it brings faith to people's hearts, to believe for the impossible; whether it is healing or a miracle, it is all from God.

> **Pastor John AD**: Healing is a desire of God. There is healing today because He wants it for all people. If He did not want to heal, He would never release healing on this earth. When you look in the Bible, you see God's passion to heal people. Not just physical healing, but also spirit, soul, and emotional healing. If there is a healing, there is an existence of God. So, Jesus healed and performed miracles to show us how God wants to heal us.

> **Apostle Les Bowling**: Our healing was paid for on the cross, in the redemption package. As our sin came upon Christ on the cross, so did our sicknesses and our infirmities. The price for our sin was paid, so

we can have faith for healing. This is one of the benefits of the New Covenant we have with God. Most believers don't struggle to believe that God forgives sins. However, we are more challenged when it comes to believing He will heal us. We all just need to remember all of it was taken care of with the finished work of Christ on the cross.

Pastor Waseem Yousaf: I love the saying, "Health is wealth." If we have health, we can enjoy all the blessings of God in our life. Health is always needed in our bodies since we live in this corruptible, sinful, and fallen world. This tormenting cycle of getting sick and then cured would break down only in eternity when we would be transferred into glorified bodies free of sickness. Healings can come from many secondary resources of this world, but the question of biblical healing directs our thoughts to three primeval sources according to the Holy Scripture:

First, healing originates from our heavenly Father, Jehovah Rapha, who declared to the Israelites, "I am the Lord, your healer" (Exodus 15:26, ESV). The Hebrew term *Rapha*, אפר, implies that only God can heal, repair, and make our bodies whole. Being the master of our bodies, He can add as well as extract any parts out of this body like a well-trained and expert technician who fixes his machine carefully.

Second, healing comes from the written Word of God as it is written, "He sent out his word and healed them" (Psalm 107:20). The Word of God has the power to heal our bodies. It also comes through the proclamation of the promises of the Bible. It works like a medicine.

Third, healing comes by claiming the work Jesus did on the cross for us, shedding his blood for our sins: "By His stripes we are healed" (Isaiah 53:5, NKJV).

Bishop Michael Pfeifer: One of Jesus' main missions was to bring God's healing and loving merciful presence to our world, to heal us physically, emotionally, psychologically and spiritually, especially from the greatest evil of sin. To free us from sin Jesus would give his life on the cross to bring God's forgiveness and mercy. Jesus focused on our hearts, because that is the main place that needs healing in the total person.

Mr. Worldwide Evangelist: Healing is probably the most misunderstood biblical principle across the entire spectrum of Christianity and the body of Christ. And yet, God gives us His divine insights through His divine Scriptures of exactly how He feels about healing. God is still doing biblical healing, or supernatural divine healing, today. God did it in Bible days; then Jesus did it throughout His ministry, in sync with the desires of Almighty God the Father. You never see Jesus doing or saying anything that would contradict healing someone. There might have been a point or two where He wanted to see where their faith was, but He never turned anyone away. Jesus never said, "It is not my will nor the will of the Father to heal you," nor did He say, "You are learning some great mystery by this sickness." The Bible says Jesus healed "all manner of sickness and all manner of disease" (Matthew 4:23, KJV), and that all those that came to Him were healed. We know everything Jesus did was the perfect will of God in action on the earth. In John 6:38, Jesus said, "I came down from heaven, not to do mine own will, but the will of him that sent me" (KJV). And so everywhere in Scripture, as Jesus ministered, he was healing.

Even the Old Testament Scriptures point toward Jesus being the healer. Look at Isaiah 53:4-5. It is so clear when Isaiah said, "He took up our pain and bore our suffering," and "He was pierced for our transgressions, he was crushed for our iniquities." The punishment that brought us peace was on Him, and "by his wounds we are healed." His blood cleansed us from all sins, but the beating and brokenness that His body endured purchased the price for what was needed for our healing. That is why holy communion is so important–the breaking of bread of communion representing the body of Christ being broken for us so we can be healed, and the wine or grape juice symbolizing His blood for the cleansing and forgiveness of sin. In those verses, He had borne our griefs and carried our sorrows, and "by his wounds we are healed."

Here's an interesting fact. When you study deeper in the actual Hebrew, the word *choliy* (חֳלִי) means "sickness, disease, and grief." Some of the modern-day diseases like E. coli are taken from the root words of what are found in the Bible. The other word found right in Isaiah, 53:4-5 is *mak'ōḇ* (בְּאֵכְמַ), and the actual meaning is "pain." It can be physical or mental pain, or pain associated with sorrow. When the verse ends by saying "by His stripes, we are healed" (NKJV), it is talking about divine healing as well. Isaiah was prophesying forward to Jesus' dying on the cross for our sins. Then in I Peter 2:24, Peter looked back in at the life and work of Jesus, culminating at the cross. Jesus Christ's sacrificial redemptive act of dying on the cross paid the price for redemption fully, ensuring the cleansing of sin first, and then the healing of the body as well as the freeing of their mind, so that we could be completely whole. We finish it out knowing in James 5:14-15 that we see the modern-day function in the church and instructions. It shows that both are part of redemption, and that healing, biblical divine healing, is for today.

Pastor Walt Landers: Jesus told all believers we are coheirs of God's kingdom with Him. We now have the same authority and power He had during his ministry on earth. So, all the healing that Jesus did, we can do and receive in the name of Jesus. We need to believe and not doubt God's promises for healing, as that belongs to us as part of our covenant right now.

Apostle Naomi Dowdy: When studying the Bible, it becomes clear Jesus brought healing to a completely new level. He made healing one of the center points of His ministry, going from town to town healing all of those who came to Him. Jesus said these healings and other signs would validate He was the Messiah, such as the lamed walked, the blind received their site and the deaf hear. For us believers, we are to follow Jesus' example and believe that healing will happen. This is the central point of our Christian belief system, and it's non-negotiable. It should be something that we expect to happen when we pray. That is the essence of faith.

In summary, healing occurred throughout the Bible and was forecasted to continue to this day through Jesus Christ's example in the New Testament. Each ministry leader interviewed for this book, including myself, has seen God bring about healing today.

Chapter 2
IF GOD LOVES US, WHY IS THERE SICKNESS?

Here are some points to consider about God and sickness:

1. Since God created us, we should never forget how much He loves us.
2. God is sovereign, and He is in control of all things.
3. The Fall of Man brought sin to the world, and with that, sickness and death.
    3a. Not all sickness is the result of our sin; however, sin can open the door for sickness.
    3b. God allows free will, and sickness can be a consequence of our disobedience.
    3c. The environment, our genetics, and how we treat our bodies can result in sickness.
4. When Satan brings sickness, we should use it to draw closer to God, and to empathize with others who are suffering.

What Does the Bible Say About This Question?

John 3:16: "For God so loved the world that he gave his one and only Son, that whoever believes in him shall not perish but have eternal life."

Romans 5:8: "But God demonstrates his own love for us in this: While we were still sinners, Christ died for us."

Isaiah 55:8-9: "'For my thoughts are not your thoughts, neither are your ways my ways,' declares the Lord. 'As the heavens are higher than the earth, so are my ways higher than your ways and my thoughts than your thoughts.'"

Romans 5:12: "Therefore, just as sin entered the world through one man [Adam], and death through sin, and in this way death came to all people, because all sinned."

John 9:1-3: "As he went along, he saw a man blind from birth. His disciples asked him, 'Rabbi, who sinned, this man or his parents, that he was born blind?' 'Neither this man nor his parents sinned,' said Jesus, 'but this happened so that the works of God might be displayed in him.'"

Psalm 38:3: "Because of your wrath there is no health in my body; there is no soundness in my bones because of my sin."

I Corinthians 11:27-30: "So then, whoever eats the bread or drinks the cup of the Lord in an unworthy manner will be guilty of sinning against the body and blood of the Lord. Everyone ought to examine themselves before they eat of the bread and drink from the cup. For those who eat and drink without discerning the body of Christ eat and drink judgment on themselves. That is why many among you are weak and sick, and a number of you have fallen asleep [in death]."

James 5:15-16a: "And the prayer offered in faith will make the sick person well; the Lord will raise them up. If they have sinned, they will be forgiven. Therefore, confess your sins to each other and pray for each other so that you may be healed."

I Corinthians 6:19-20: "Do you not know that your bodies are temples of the Holy Spirit, who is in you, whom you have received from God? You are not your own; you were bought at a price. Therefore honor God with your bodies."

Job 2:6-7: "The Lord said to Satan. "Very well, then, he [Job] is in your hands; but you must spare his life." So Satan went out from the presence of the Lord and afflicted Job with painful sores from the soles of his feet to the crown of his head."

Job 42:12a: "The Lord blessed the latter part of Job's life more than the former part."

Job 42:16-17: "After this, Job lived a hundred and forty years; he saw his children and their children to the fourth generation. And so Job died, an old man and full of years."

2 Corinthians 12:9: "But he [the Lord] said to me, 'My grace is sufficient for you, for my power is made perfect in weakness.' Therefore I will boast all the more gladly about my weaknesses, so that Christ's power may rest on me."

Let's Look Deeper:

It is difficult to understand how and why there is sickness in our world when we have a God Who loves us. This is a common question from both believers and nonbelievers and does not have an easy answer. Let's walk through each point one by one:

1. God loves us.
There are many places in the Bible where God shows His love for all of us, regardless of if we love and follow Him in return. Most people are familiar with John 3:16 telling us that God loved us so much he sent His Son Jesus to die for us. Romans 5:8 tells a similar story, highlighting that even though we sin, God will always love us. Regardless of where you are in your walk to, with, or away from the Lord, know and remember He loves you.

2. God is sovereign.
We will never fully understand all the reasons for sickness, not until we meet God face-to-face. We need to accept God is sovereign, which means He has ultimate authority and answers to no one. He is the King of Kings and Lord of Lords. He oversees all things, from the vastness of the stars

to the number of hairs on our heads (Matthew 10:30). He does what He wants in His time, and we do not always have the answers. When we recognize and accept God's sovereignty, then even in our most difficult circumstances, we can trust that all He does is for our ultimate good. God tells us, "For I know the plans I have for you . . . plans to prosper you and not to harm you, plans to give you hope and a future" (Jeremiah 29:11). He sees the big picture, including things we will never see nor understand. So, we cannot always understand His ways (Isaiah 55:8-9). He sees all things, and all things operate in His timing, in accordance with His will.

3. It was Adam's first sin (the Fall of Man) that brought sickness and death to the world through Satan.
We currently live in a world full of problems, trials, sickness, and death. None of this existed in the Garden of Eden before sin entered the world through Adam and Eve (Romans 5:12). It was man's sin that allowed our enemy Satan to bring sickness and disease to the world.

It is important to remember that Jesus' death on the cross, and His resurrection, defeated the forces of evil. He provided the solution to sickness and death. We are all sinners in need of a Savior, and that is Jesus Christ. Becoming a believer does not mean you will never experience sickness, injury, or death, but it provides assurance that Jesus will always be with you, even through the most difficult times. God still loves all the people on this earth and seeks for every one of them to come to Him, through His Son Jesus Christ. See the appendix for more information on becoming a believer.

a. Not every sickness is due to sin, but sin can open the door for sickness in our lives.
In reviewing John 9:1-3, we learn that not every ailment comes from sin. Jesus' disciples asked who had sinned for the man to be born blind, him or his parents? Jesus said, "Neither this man nor his parents sinned," which shows us not all sickness is related to sin. In this case, Jesus explained why: "This happened so that the works of God might be displayed in him." Jesus told us that the reason for this man's blindness was so that He could be an example for others to see the power of God's healing.

However, there are many Bible verses that point to a correlation between sin and sickness. In Psalm 38:3, King David linked his physical suffering directly to his sins. Many scholars believe David wrote this psalm as a lament to the Lord over his affair with Bathsheba and subsequent decision to send his loyal servant Uriah (her husband) to be killed in battle. We also see this correlation in the story of Jesus healing the paralyzed man. Instead of proclaiming the paralyzed man be healed, Jesus said, "Your sins are forgiven" (the story is found in Matthew 9:2; Mark 2:5; and Luke 5:20). In a different healing situation, a short time after Jesus healed a crippled man from the Bethesda pool, Jesus found him at the temple and said to him, "See, you are well again. Stop sinning or something worse may happen to you" (John 5:14).

We receive a stern warning against leading a sinful life from Paul in 1 Corinthians 11:27-30. Paul pointed out that if we take communion in an unworthy manner, with active sin in our lives, the result will be physical consequences like weakness, sickness, or even death.

> **Mr. Worldwide Evangelist:** There is a relationship between sin and sickness. James 5:15-16 shows the importance of confessing our sins. Not only will we recover and be healed, but it says if we have committed sins, the Lord will forgive us. That is powerful, as it shows that both are part of redemption, and that biblical divine healing is for today.

b. Our free will choices and disobedience to God's Word can result in sickness. The Old Testament is full of stories of the consequences God's people faced due to their free will and disobedient choices. In those days, the Lord gave 613 strict commands for His people to follow. When they sinned, there were consequences, which typically included sickness. God promised to protect the Israelites from disease if they obeyed His commands (Exodus 15:26). This promise implies disobedience could lead to illness. One example is found in Numbers 12:10, when Miriam was struck with leprosy for slandering her brother Moses, who was leading Israel at that time. Miriam suffered sickness due to the consequences of her sin but was later restored after Moses requested her healing from the Lord.

In the New Testament, Jesus rejected many of the man-made and burdensome rules that religious leaders of the past enforced on the Jewish people. However, He did not reject His followers' right to choose their own actions and path in life. Just like in biblical times, God does not force us to follow Him but gives us free will; and just like our spiritual ancestors, we will also face consequences if we do not follow God's commands. Jesus simply asks us, "If you love me, keep my commands" (John 14:15).

c. The environment, our genetics, and how we treat our bodies can result in sickness.
We are all blessed with the amazing bodies the Lord provides for us, and we need to take good care of them. In 1 Corinthians 6:19-20, Paul explained how important it is to treat our bodies well. Our bodies are a temple of the Holy Spirit, because as believers the Holy Spirit lives in us and through us.

Sadly, due to the nature of our sinful and fallen world, there are environmental conditions that affect our bodies. I grew up in a very industrial area of Michigan, which had higher than normal rates of cancers, especially pancreatic cancer. All the rivers close to my house were polluted, and we weren't allowed to swim in them due to the harmful chemicals. I was later told there was a good chance our drinking water had been contaminated by those chemicals, which could have been the root cause of both my mom and I developing pancreatic cancer. All of us have the possibility of being exposed to harmful chemicals through our air, food, water, homes, or materials we are exposed to at work. In some cases, there is not much we can do other than pray for protection and relief. If you have the means and ability, removing yourself from a harmful environment can be a difficult but necessary step to maintain the physical health of yourself and your family, but unfortunately this is not always possible.

In addition, there are genetic conditions and predispositions that are passed down through family lines. These range from mental health conditions, such as depression or substance use disorder, to physical conditions, such as heart disease or cancer. I personally suffer the same arthritis as both my mother and maternal grandmother, and I am praying that it does not get passed to my daughter. We can pray to break these chains of physical and mental problems in the name of Jesus.

We should do our best to live well, eat well, sleep well, and exercise. Yet, when we live an unhealthily lifestyle, we can expect consequences. Paul wrote in 1 Timothy 4:8 that "physical training is of some value." Decades of medical literature have shown us that smoking, excessive alcohol, and poor diet lead to chronic medical conditions that are often irreversible. When we live an unhealthy lifestyle, we can expect direct consequences. We cannot blame God for the things we do to our own bodies; instead, we need to remain cognizant of what lifestyle choices may be affecting our health.

I have had to live with some physical consequences of my lifestyle choices. I struggled for years with painful knee arthritis. I went through five years of trying every type of injection my doctor had to offer. I prayed often for healing and relief, thinking the Lord would miraculously heal me just like he did with my pancreatic cancer. However, I ended up having a total knee replacement on my right knee in 2017. So, healing of my constant pain came through a medical procedure and physical therapy. When I asked the Lord why I was not miraculously healed in my knee, He told me the acceleration of my arthritis was a consequence of my extreme sports lifestyle when I was younger—running, skydiving, mountain biking, extreme downhill skiing, scuba diving, and being a catcher in a softball league for many years. I accepted this answer from the Lord and understand that there are natural consequences of prior decisions that degrade our bodies. I am so glad I had those amazing experiences and wouldn't exchange them even if it meant I would never have had knee pain. I am grateful now that I am pain free and the knee replacement hasn't limited my active lifestyle.

4. Sickness should draw people to God and help us empathize with others.
I do not believe God "makes" people sick, or that He has some "angel of illness" He uses to zap people with sickness. However, I believe when Satan brings sickness upon us, we should use that trial to draw us closer to God and to serve as a catalyst for spiritual reflection to determine if we are living a righteous life. Sickness can show us our dependence on God and will encourage us to seek His comfort and healing. A great biblical example is the story of Job. Satan took away all he had, except his wife (Job 1:11-22), and inflicted him from head to toe with painful sores in Job 2:6-7. Reading through Job shows us a man who stayed faithful to God throughout his trial and suffering. In the end, we see in Job 42:12a and 16-17, God healed him and blessed him with more than he had before his trial. Job provides a great example of being faithful to God, regardless of what Satan throws us.

For many of us, there are times we don't understand why we have not received quick healing, or why we remain in pain. We need to remember

God's grace through our weakness, and that Jesus is with us during our suffering, as Paul tells us in 2 Corinthians 12:9. In 2023, I fell and suffered a displaced fracture on my dominant writing arm. I was blessed that my daughter Leia, who is an emergency medicine doctor, was with me when it happened. She splinted my wrist and got me to the hospital quickly. The fracture and subsequent surgery were both very painful, especially since I could not tolerate any prescription pain medicine. I prayed for relief, which came slowly but eventually. I did not understand why I had to endure weeks of terrible pain.

The next month, I went on a short-term mission trip to Pakistan. The day we arrived, my main contact, Pastor John AD, asked me to go to the home of a man who had just been in a vehicle accident. When I arrived at the man's home to pray with him, I discovered he also had fractured his dominant arm. It was going to be another two weeks before he could have the surgery he needed, and he was not given any pain medicine. I had so much empathy for this man's exact suffering. I prayed for him, through a translator, with all the power and authority from the Lord, along with the knowledge of the pain I had just gone through. I knew his pain and knew exactly how to pray. By the time I finished praying, the translator said the injured man no longer had any pain; praise the Lord! I do not know how long he stayed pain free, but I believe the Lord was with him through his surgery and recovery. I do not believe the Lord caused my wrist injury and intentionally caused my pain, but the Lord used me and my experience of suffering to pray with empathy, knowledge, and authority for this man.

> **Pastor Walt Landers put the question of sickness into a good perspective:**
>
> What about the children who suffer? Or those who lived a good life having love and compassion for others, but died too young? Even if God told us why, it probably would not be good enough for us to fully understand the reasons. Often, we don't have the answers. We must make sure that doubt doesn't overcome our faith. If we're asking "why," we are asking the wrong question.
>
> There are so many things that happen to all of us throughout our lives. We know and believe that our God is a good God. We know that "God anointed Jesus of Nazareth with the Holy Spirit and power, and how he went around doing good and healing all who were under

> the power of the devil, because God was with him" (Acts 10:38). So, I continually declare my God is a good God. My fight is with "the thief [who] comes only to steal and kill and destroy" (John 10:10), and that is Satan. There are demonic attacks and evil forces all around us, because we live in a fallen world. This also means we're exposed to toxins and all types of harmful things. To be honest, most of us know (but may not admit to ourselves) we don't always eat the best or do the recommended amount of exercise in our lives. This allows our immune system to become compromised, which can make it easier for sickness to come on us and others.
>
> I plan to step into glory fighting the fight of faith and trust in Jesus, that He is healing. I am thankful that I was taught early on some of these truths and the power of believing and confessing the Word and fighting that fight of faith.

In summary, Jesus overcame the world and is always here for us. Jesus said, "I have told you these things, so that in me you may have peace. In this world you will have trouble. But take heart! I have overcome the world" (John 16:33). Regardless of the troubles we are facing, Jesus is walking with us every step of the way.

Chapter 3
WHO ACTUALLY DOES THE HEALING?

OUR FATHER GOD DOES THE HEALING. WE CAN BE BLESSED WHEN the Lord uses us to bring forth healing in others, but the credit and glory go to God alone.

In addition, we are not to judge when, why, and how the Lord heals His people. God heals in His way, and in His timing.

What Does the Bible Say About This Question?
Exodus 15:26b: "For I am the LORD, who heals you."

Isaiah 38:21: "Isaiah had said, 'Prepare a poultice of figs and apply it to the boil, and he will recover.'"

Matthew 4:23: "Jesus went throughout Galilee, teaching in their synagogues, proclaiming the good news of the kingdom, and healing every disease and sickness among the people."

John 14:13-14: "And I will do whatever you ask in my name, so that the Father may be glorified in the Son. You may ask me for anything in my name, and I will do it."

Let's Look Deeper:
1. God does the healing.
The Bible makes it clear in Exodus 15:26, it is our Father God who does the healing. This short but definitive verse is the first in the Bible that specifically

mentions healing. There are many healings in the Old Testament, which makes it clear that God is the ultimate healer, though at times He does so through the actions of others. For example, King Hezekiah became ill and was at the point of death, so he prayed to the Lord asking for healing. God used the Prophet Isaiah to tell King Hezekiah how to recover from his illness using a poultice of figs (Isaiah 38:21).

In the New Testament, Jesus demonstrated God's power for healing as well. It is difficult to pinpoint Jesus' first healing, though most scholars agree it was after His baptism and forty-day fast in the wilderness. We know early in His ministry, Jesus healed Mary Magdalene of seven demons, as she was one of His early followers. Jesus' first recorded biblical healing is in Luke 4:35-36, when He healed a man being possessed by an evil spirit in Galilee. Jesus went on to heal many others.

Healing was easy for Jesus, with the power and authority He received from His Father to do His works on the earth. In Matthew 4:23, we see Jesus going to numerous synagogues, healing everyone He encountered.

Jesus told His disciples the work He was doing was to reveal His Father God to us. In John 14:9b, Jesus said, "Anyone who has seen me has seen the Father." So, we see God's character in the work of Jesus. However, Jesus also made it clear that His work was to glorify the works of the Father, for God's glory, and not to take the credit for himself. We see in John 14:13-14 that when we ask in His name (the name of Jesus), the Father is glorified through His Son. Jesus never took the glory for the miracles He did, but honored His Father God.

When the Lord uses us to bring out healing in someone, we need to ensure God alone receives the credit. There will be times when someone is healed while you are praying for them, and they will want to thank *you* for healing them. Be quick to give the glory to God, and tell those who were healed to praise and thank God for their healing. Do not let pride take ahold of you, as we need to remain humble when we are being used by God to heal others. We should always remain grateful to God when He uses us to facilitate His healing. If we take the glory from God, He will most likely take away our ability to bring about His healing.

2. God heals in His way and in His timing.

An important point to remember is even if we are used by the Lord for healing, don't know the big picture of who, when or why He heals. We know Jesus healed all who came to Him, regardless of their sins, and He never turned anyone away. Healing is part of the new covenant when Jesus died on the cross for our sins, reconciling us to God, and giving us eternal life. We will never know the big picture of how God is working in people's lives and the process He is using to heal them. Our role is to pray and believe in faith for healing.

> **Pastor Lisa Chin:** We need to remember only God knows whether the person is going to be healed instantaneously or later. My responsibility is to pray in faith and trust God for healing.

> **Superintendent Aaron Hlavin:** I have a great story where God taught me about His will regarding healing. Around 2015, I was visiting another church and praying for people after the church service. First, a mom and her son came up for prayer. As I prayed for them, I could tell the kid was not happy to be up there and was not engaged in the prayer. I think his mom dragged him up to the altar, and she was hoping and praying for his healing. During the prayer, I didn't feel any move of the Holy Spirit and didn't see any evidence of immediate healing. So, I moved on to pray for another person who was really crying out to God. This person was so emotional and passionate for God and cried out for healing. I was really hoping for their healing but later discovered they did not get healed and ended up passing away. Years later, I ran into that mom, and she said, "You prayed for my son, and he was healed." Then, it was this juxtaposition in my mind of her son, who did not appear like he wanted healing, being forced to the altar by his mom. But he needed healing, and he was healed. It reminded me of my spiritual immaturity at that time. No matter how long you have been in ministry, you have these moments where you realize you got it wrong. Then God said to me, "You are focused on healing in the wrong mindset. You have no idea when you are praying for someone what I am doing. So just pray. Your assignment is to pray. It is my assignment to do the work." So, we need to get our eyes back on Who's the healer, not who does the praying.

These words from **Superintendent Hlavin** provide a great summary:

The church needs to focus more on the grandness of God, and celebrate any healing that comes from God and not the person who prayed for healing. I think in America, and maybe other places around the world, we are bad at celebrating Jesus. When we receive healing, we make it more about the person who prayed for us than glorifying Jesus. We need to get back to Jesus. God uses people. God uses moments. God uses miracles. God performs the gift of healing, but it is Jesus, Jesus, Jesus.

Chapter 4

CAN ANYONE PRAY FOR HEALING?

Yes, anyone can pray for healing; however, the most effective prayers are done through believers in Jesus Christ. All believers can and should pray for others.

The prayers of a righteous believer are powerful.

We are not to judge who is worthy to be used by God to pray for others.

What Does the Bible Say About This Question?

I Thessalonians 5:25: "Brothers and sisters, pray for us."

I Timothy 2:I: "I urge, then, first of all, that petitions, prayers, intercession and thanksgiving be made for all people."

Matthew 5:44: "But I tell you, love your enemies and pray for those who persecute you."

Matthew 14:14: "When Jesus landed and saw a large crowd, he had compassion on them and healed their sick."

Mark 16:17-18: "And these signs will accompany those who believe: In my name they will drive out demons; they will speak in new tongues; they will pick up snakes with their hands; and when they drink deadly poison, it will not hurt them at all; they will place their hands on sick people, and they will get well."

Luke 10:1: "After this the Lord appointed seventy-two others and sent them two by two ahead of him to every town and place where he was about to go."

Matthew 10:1: "Jesus called his twelve disciples to him and gave them authority to drive out impure spirits and to heal every disease and sickness."

Romans 8:17: "Now if we are children, then we are heirs–heirs of God and co-heirs with Christ, if indeed we share in his sufferings in order that we may also share in his glory."

1 John 5:14-15: "This is the confidence we have in approaching God: that if we ask anything according to his will, he hears us. And if we know that he hears us–whatever we ask–we know that we have what we asked of him."

James 5:16b: "The prayer of a righteous person is powerful and effective."

Mark 9:38-40: "'Teacher,' said John, 'we saw someone driving out demons in your name and we told him to stop, because he was not one of us.' 'Do not stop him,' Jesus said. 'For no one who does a miracle in my name can in the next moment say anything bad about me, for whoever is not against us is for us.'"

Let's Look Deeper:
1. All believers can and should pray for others.
Anyone can pray for healing for other people. However, the followers of Jesus Christ who believe Jesus still heals today have an important role to pray for others. This was mentioned by everyone who was interviewed for this book.

All believers should pray for others. Paul wrote about this in many places. First, he asked for prayer in 1 Thessalonians 5:25, then, in 1 Timothy 2:1, he told us we should be praying for all people. Jesus told us to pray not only for each other, but for our enemies as well (Matthew 5:44). All these verses point to the responsibility all believers have to pray for others.

Healing, at its essence, is an act of compassion. Jesus demonstrated this compassion in Matthew 14:14. We should pray for people to be healed because we care about the sick and want them to feel better. We should not pray for people to be healed to demonstrate some power we have over them, as that is arrogant and prideful. To be used by God as a healer, we must have a commitment to helping others, like nurses and doctors in the medical profession. We should feel a responsibility to pray for a person's spirit, soul, and body to return to health.

> **Pastor John AD:** God performed many miracles through believers. The moment the person receives and accepts Jesus Christ, they have the power of the Lord, a gift of God. So, the moment when a person receives Christ, they can pray for healing.

> **Missionary Jared Dietrich:** We need to encourage all believers to lay hands on people and pray for healing. Don't let anyone get the idea that the pastor is the only one that can do it; all believers can and should minister healing.

> **Bishop Michael Pfeifer:** We are called by the Spirit to go out and be healers in the name of Jesus. The Bible is filled with the healing presence of our God, and this healing was one of the great gifts that Jesus gave to His Church. Jesus Christ fulfilled all the Old Testament messianic promises of deliverance and freedom, and as already mentioned, brought us God's mercy, forgiveness and healing, especially to free us from the terrible evil of sin. All His followers are invited to share in this same wonderful gift.

> **Pastor Waseem Yousaf:** Prayer is another big source for healing miracles in our lives. When we come to God through the channel of prayer and ask God according to the biblical promises, healing occurs in our lives. During prayer, we use anointed oil, prayer cloths, water, and laying hands on people. We can see these practices in the book of Acts. These ways of healing can be used even in our modern times.

Mr. Worldwide Evangelist: Scripture tells us the common believer can lay hands on the sick and witness the sick being healed by the power of God. It is through the power of Jesus, and the authority that Jesus has given His church to pray in this way, as found in Mark 16:17-18, KJV. This is part of Jesus' Great Commission, right after He said to go into all the world and preach the Gospel, the Good News, to every creature. Then, the Word mentions the miracles we can do in Jesus' name, including "lay hands on the sick, and they [the sick] shall recover."

Superintendent Aaron Hlavin: People get confused when they think they must have a special gift of healing to pray for someone to get healed. I remember people at our church would come to me during worship and say, "Pastor, this person needs prayer for healing," and I would say, "So go pray for him." They'd say, "But you're the pastor." I would have to tell them that not every pastor has the Spiritual Gifts of Healing, just because they are the pastor. God is not going to stop healing somebody who is praying in earnest because they don't have the Spiritual Gifts of Healing. Too often, the church has created their own hierarchy of who can do what, when really we all just need to focus on Jesus.

Jesus modeled this lack of a healing hierarchy for us in the New Testament. He did not heal alone, but had many followers, which He called "disciples" or students. In Luke 10:1, Jesus selected seventy-two of His followers to go into every town He was about to enter into to prepare the way. Later, Jesus designated twelve of these disciples as apostles or "sent ones." We see in Matthew 10:1, Jesus gave His twelve disciples all power and authority to drive out impure spirits and to heal every disease and sickness.

Our role is to be like Jesus. Believers need to understand they have the same authority as Jesus Christ to heal any sickness. It is part of the Christian lifestyle to pray for one another. Prayer can be for all needs but should include healings.

Today, all believers are heirs of God and coheirs with Jesus Christ (Romans 8:17). This means believers have the same power and authority as Jesus. The Lord uses us to pray and speak His words of healing to ourselves and others. John 14:14, which we discussed in chapter 3, tells us when we ask for things in the name of Jesus, He will do it. We just need to ask according to His will and not just our will. Reviewing I John 5:14-15 explains our prayers must align with the principles and commands found in the Word of God, not just our own desires and wants.

So, if you are a believer, just do it! All believers have the power to heal and should feel empowered to learn about the spiritual gifts. You don't need to start out holding a prayer service; start small and practice. Pray for yourself, for your pets, for your family and friends. A person who strongly believes in the power of God, and knows their authority is in Him, has the faith to heal through Jesus Christ.

2. The prayers of a righteous believer are powerful and effective.

Let's take our responsibility to pray to a deeper level. When we accept Jesus into our lives, confess our sins, and repent, we become believers. However, to remain righteous, we need to free ourselves from sin and stay away from temptation.

This does not only refer to pastors, but to all believers. If you are actively sinning, then you are not righteous. If you feel guilty, shameful, or convicted about how you are living and acting right now, then you are not righteous before the Lord. Stop everything you are doing and pray to Jesus; ask for forgiveness for your sins and truly repent. After this, you must take action and make a real change in your life to avoid that sin again.

> **Pastor Jim Westheim**: When we live sinful lives, acting out against God's direction in the Bible, we are not righteous. When we read James 5:16b, it points out, "The prayer of a righteous person is powerful and effective."

> **Bishop Michael Pfeifer**: When we are righteous and living in God's grace and love, there is so much we can do empowered by the Holy Spirit to help all of God's children. When we follow Jesus faithfully, beginning with the call to Holiness in our baptism, we are called to go out and be holy healers in His name, especially to help them grow in a loving relationship with Christ. As righteous believers and followers of Christ, Jesus wants us to reach out to others who are suffering in any way, and pray and work for care and healing for these people.

3. We should not judge who is following Jesus and healing in His name.
Take note of the story in Mark 9:38-40. Jesus' disciples wanted to stop people who were outside their group from praying for and healing others. Jesus was quick to correct them, saying anyone who was healing in His name was aligned with them in faith.

We should be careful not to stand in judgment against other people. We can never truly know the status of their current relationship with God. Some people may have deep faith in their hearts but are less comfortable with specific labels such as "born-again believer." We need to be careful not to pass judgment like the disciples did in Mark 9. Never discourage someone from praying. Let God alone be their judge.

> **Missionary Mary:** Sometimes the church disqualifies people that Jesus does not disqualify.

In summary, as a believer, you should pray for people whenever possible and always add healing to your prayers. Check to ensure your life is right with God, or your healing prayers may lack efficacy. Support and encourage all who want to pray for healing in others. Do not judge anyone's standing or righteousness before God.

Chapter 5
WHAT IS THE MOST IMPORTANT THING NEEDED FOR HEALING?

F AITH IS THE MOST IMPORTANT THING NEEDED FOR HEALING, FOR BOTH the healer and the person being healed.

When we trust in the Lord and pray for the Spiritual Gift of Faith, we will see greater healings and miracles.

What Does the Bible Say About This Question?

James 5:15: "And the prayer offered in faith will make the sick person well; the Lord will raise them up. If they have sinned, they will be forgiven."

James 1:6-7: "But when you ask, you must believe and not doubt, because the one who doubts is like a wave of the sea, blown and tossed by the wind. That person should not expect to receive anything from the Lord."

Romans 8:2: "Because through Christ Jesus the law of the Spirit who gives life has set you free from the law of sin and death."

I Corinthians 12:1, 4-11: "Now about the gifts of the Spirit, brothers and sisters, I do not want you to be uninformed. . . . There are different kinds of gifts, but the same Spirit distributes them. There are different kinds of service, but the same Lord. There are different kinds of working, but in all of them and in everyone it is the same God at work. Now to each one the manifestation of the Spirit is given for the common good. To one there is given through the Spirit a message of wisdom, to another a message of knowledge by means of the same Spirit, to another *faith* by the same Spirit, to another *gifts of healing* by that one Spirit, to another miraculous powers, to another prophecy, to another distinguishing between spirits, to another speaking in different kinds of tongues, and to still another the interpretation of tongues. All these are the work of one and the same Spirit, and he distributes them to each one, just as he determines." (emphasis added)

Luke 22:19-20: "And he took bread, gave thanks and broke it, and gave it to them, saying, 'This is my body given for you; do this in remembrance of me.' In the same way, after the supper he took the cup, saying, 'This cup is the new covenant in my blood, which is poured out for you.'"

Matthew 8:10: "Truly I [Jesus] tell you, I have not found anyone in Israel with such great faith."

Mark 5:34: "Daughter, your faith has healed you. Go in peace and be freed from your suffering."

Mark 10:51-52: "'What do you want me to do for you?' Jesus asked him. The blind man said, 'Rabbi, I want to see.' 'Go,' said Jesus, 'your faith has healed you.' Immediately he received his sight and followed Jesus along the road."

Matthew 13:58: "And he [Jesus] did not do many miracles there because of their lack of faith."

Let's Look Deeper:
1. All individuals who desire to pray for healing for others must have faith.

Faith is the most important factor contributing to your success on the journey of learning to bring healing to others through Jesus. This book has already highlighted that all believers have the same power and authority that Jesus had for healing. Now, you must believe that the Lord will use you to pray for and bring comfort to others. We should use the same faith described in James 5:15 when praying for others. We also need to walk out James 1:6-7, not allowing doubt when we ask for things from the Lord.

Mr. Worldwide Evangelist: It is important for us to be "agents of faith" concerning the power of God. We are extensions of both heaven's glory and manifestation on this earth. Knowing that we carry a spirit of faith takes the burden for healing off the person we are praying for. Yes, they can be growing in the Word of God and having faith to believe God for healing. But it is our responsibility as ministers and believers to carry that attitude and spirit of faith, to lift people up out of where they are and bring them closer to God. We should be the ones that bring the power of God in this situation right then and there.

This power of God is demonstrated in a great story from the early 1900s about Missionary John G. Lake. He had a revelation of God's power and believed he carried the life of God in him that could drive out sickness and disease because these are forms of death. There is a well-documented story of Missionary Lake ministering to many during the horrible and deadly bubonic plague that swept through South Africa. When medical teams and scientists arrived, they could not understand how Lake was unaffected by the plague. Lake said, "Take the bloody trough off that dead individual's mouth, and put the germs on my hand." The doctors watched under a microscope as the bubonic plague germs touched his hand, then instantly died. When they asked Lake what his secret was, he said, "It is the law of the Spirit of life in Christ, as Jesus has made me free from the law of sin and death." If we have the life of God in us, we also have the law of the Spirit of life as seen in Romans 8:2. In Christ, we were made free from the law of sin and death, so when we are operating in that law of life, we know it drives out sickness and disease. However, I implore you to exercise caution and use wisdom when you are praying for people with contagious illnesses.

We can pray for healing in others in the saving faith we received when we became believers. Healing is only one of nine gifts of the Holy Spirit that Paul told us we can claim, and we will discuss this in depth in the next chapter. The verses in 1 Corinthians 12:4-11 list the different gifts of the Holy Spirit. Paul wrote how important it is to understand these gifts, (1 Corinthians 12:1) and to know the Lord has given all believers at least one gift to do His work here on earth. Acts 2:3 gives a vivid picture of when the Holy Spirit came upon Jesus' early followers as "tongues of fire." These gifts were not just for Jesus' disciples, but for all believers as well. Some people operate in one or multiple of these gifts all the time; for others, each gift can come and go according to the Lord's plan for their ministry. These gifts of the Holy Spirit flow through people when needed for God's mission and work. I have flowed in most of these Holy Spirit gifts at one time or another in my ministry. There are many good books available for further study on all nine of the gifts of the Holy Spirit (such as *Discover Your Spiritual Gifts*, by C. Peter Wagner), but our focus in this chapter is on the importance of the Spiritual Gift of Faith, and how to secure it.

> **Pastor Didier Kokora:** Here are some good steps for all believers:
> - To diligently seek the Holy Spirit and His work, allowing them to experience a personal Pentecost.
> - To study, understand, and practice of spiritual gifts as outward demonstrations of God's power.
> - Encourage other believers to be filled with the fruit of the Spirit, which is the character of Jesus Christ, in order to prepare the next generation to carry the torch of faith forward.

If you want the Lord to use you to operate in healings and miracles, it is important to first ask for the Spiritual Gift of Faith. That is not the simple faith of belief in Jesus. It is a supernatural outpouring from the Holy Spirit to believers that enables them to sustain an unwavering trust in God for what is needed at that time. Once we have the Spiritual Gift of Faith, then we know we will have the *added strength* for God to use us to bring forth healings and miracles in His name. Many times the Holy Spirit has prompted me to pray for an increase in faith right before a huge trial in my life, or a missions trip where I witnessed a large outpouring of healings and miracles.

> **Director Jill Boyonas:** I have the Spiritual Gift of Faith, and when that gift rises in me, healing happens. Whenever the gift of Faith manifests I feel a holy boldness rises within me and this boldness gives me the feeling that I can do all things through Christ. The first time I experienced this was when my four-year-old daughter had fever for almost a week and it wouldn't let up, even with medication. One night I woke up with my daughter crying in pain. Then suddenly this holy boldness rose up from within me and when I rebuked the fever my daughter was instantly healed.

The Spiritual Gift of Faith is also very valuable when praying for and believing in healing for ourselves. Simply proclaim in faith that you are healed. A good practice to follow is taking communion when praying for yourself for healing. Just make sure you confess your sins first so you know you are in right standing with God.

> **Apostle Lana Heightley:** I believe that taking communion brings healing. People should practice communion in their home, especially for illnesses or injuries that require a long recovery. In Luke 22:19-20, Jesus declared the bread was His body, and it is very symbolic when you tie it to His work on the cross. The stripes He bore and the death He suffered were for us and our sins, so taking communion is in remembrance of that sacrifice. We can claim healing when we take the bread in faith for healing. I take communion every day, and I confess the promises that come with that, which include complete body healing as well as soul healing. So, at home you can take that wherever you want in remembrance of him.

A strong biblical example of the faith required for healing is the centurion, found in Matthew 8:5-13. This faithful Roman commander approached Jesus, asking Him to heal his sick servant at home. He understood authority and knew Jesus only had to "say the word" and his servant would be healed. Jesus told him, "Truly I tell you, I have not found anyone in Israel with such great faith" (Matthew 8:10). This story emphasizes that healing can still happen through faith, even when the distance between the sick and the healer is far. Jesus was amazed by the centurion's faith, a wonderful spiritual goal to which we should all aspire.

2. Having faith is also important for those desiring healing.
A fundamental principle for those who want healing is that they should have faith to believe they can be healed by God. Many times in the Bible, people were healed just because of their faith. We don't see many examples of people healed without first having the faith to believe the healing would happen.

> **Missionary Jared Dietrich:** Jesus is not going to heal someone who does not want healing or does not believe they can be healed.

The story of the poor woman who had been bleeding for many years is a great example of faith in action. The story is important as it is found in Matthew 9, Mark 5, and Luke 8. This woman believed in Jesus' healing power but felt she was not worthy to ask for it. She was constantly bleeding (most scholars believe it was menstrual bleeding), so she was unclean in the eyes of the Jewish people. At the time, no one was allowed to touch women during their menstrual cycle or they would be "unclean," requiring a lengthy purification ritual to become "clean" again. This woman lived a lonely and isolated life, which is why she silently came up behind Jesus. She just wanted to touch the tassel of his outer garment, knowing the blue in the tassel represented the Word of God. This is such a great example of true faith and determination. When she finally reached that tassel, Jesus felt the healing power leave Him. He turned and told her, "Daughter, your faith has healed you. Go in peace and be freed from your suffering" (Mark 5:34). Her absolute faith in His power resulted in her healing.

Another example is the story of Blind Bartimaeus in Mark 10:51-52. Bartimaeus heard about Jesus and had the faith to be healed. However, he had to yell at the top of his lungs to be heard over the crowds. Jesus' disciples dismissed him, but not Jesus. Jesus called him over, and Bartimaeus threw off his begging cloak. In that action, he demonstrated he would no longer need that cloak for begging. It was that faith, and his belief in Jesus, that healed him.

There is only one example in the Bible, Matthew 13:58, where it is mentioned that Jesus could not do healings or miracles due to a lack of faith, and that was in His hometown. These people saw Jesus only as the son of Joseph, the carpenter, and they could not believe or accept He was anything more. They did not have the faith for healing.

As we finish this chapter, it is important to know that faith is important for both the person praying for healing and the person desiring healing. With strong faith, we can believe for healing for our own bodies and have the faith to heal others, even those who are away from our presence.

Chapter 6
ARE THERE DIFFERENT WAYS TO BRING HEALING?

Y ES, THERE ARE TWO MAIN WAYS TO HEAL MENTIONED IN THE BIBLE. First is by the healing faith given to all Christians.

Second is with the Holy Spirit Gifts of Healing as mentioned in 1 Corinthians 12. These spiritual healing gifts flow through select believers as the Holy Spirit determines they are needed.

What Does the Bible Say About This Question?

Acts 3:16: "By faith in the name of Jesus, this man whom you see and know was made strong. It is Jesus' name and the faith that comes through him that has completely healed him, as you can all see."

Ephesians 4:11-12: "So Christ himself gave the apostles, the prophets, the evangelists, the pastors and teachers, to equip his people for works of service, so that the body of Christ may be built up."

I Corinthians 12:1, 4-11: "Now about the gifts of the Spirit, brothers and sisters, I do not want you to be uninformed.... There are different kinds of gifts, but the same Spirit distributes them. There are different kinds of service, but the same Lord. There are different kinds of working, but in all of them and in everyone it is the same God at work. Now to each one the manifestation of the Spirit is given for the common good. To one there is given through the Spirit a message of wisdom, to another a message of knowledge by means of the same Spirit, to another faith by the same Spirit, to another gifts of healing by that one Spirit, to another miraculous powers, to another prophecy, to another distinguishing between spirits, to another speaking in different kinds of tongues, and to still another the interpretation of tongues. All these are the work of one and the same Spirit, and he distributes them to each one, just as he determines."

Let's Look Deeper:

There are two types of healing referenced in the Bible. The first is for any believer who has the faith to believe in healing. Look at Acts 3:16, as the man was healed by faith when Peter spoke healing in the name of Jesus over him. This faith was discussed in detail in chapter 5.

The second type of healing is through the Holy Spirit or Spiritual Gifts of Healing Paul wrote about in 1 Corinthians 12. Before explaining the Spiritual Gifts of Healing, it is important to first understand how the Lord set up His church. In Ephesians 4:11-12, Paul detailed the offices or positions the Lord set up for His church. Those are apostles, prophets, evangelists, pastors, and teachers. Normally these individuals perform full-time work for the Lord, to build up and equip the church. The Bible never mentions there is a specific office of "healer."

> **Superintendent Aaron Hlavin:** Once a guy came up to me at a church, right after I became the superintendent of the Michigan Network of Assemblies of God. He said, "I am kind of concerned about the Assemblies of God. Who is the 'healer' in the Assemblies of God?" And I said, "Jesus." He replied, "No, no, no, who is the 'person' I go to where I will get healed." I said, "The fact that you are chasing a person is wrong. Yes, some people have those Gifts of Healing, and God works through them, but it has never been 'that person.'" We need to focus on Jesus and be blessed when He heals through us.

It is important to understand what makes the Gifts of Healing by the Holy Spirit unique. They are a supernatural healing of injuries or diseases without natural means of any sort. The Gifts of Healing flow through certain believers, either continuously or on occasion when it is needed. These Gifts of Healing are seen mostly in individuals who hold the office of Evangelist, who use these gifts to bring the supernatural presence of the Lord to meetings and gatherings. There are people who operate in the Gifts of Healing regularly, but it's not a church office.

> **Mr. Worldwide Evangelist:** Here's an interesting point about the gifts of the Holy Spirit in I Corinthians 12: only one of the nine gifts listed is in a plural form, and that is "Gifts of Healing." Paul, the writer of Corinthians, listed the other eight gifts of the Holy Spirit as singular gifts. I believe because there are so many different forms of sickness and disease on the earth, God has given this huge, broad gift category of the Gifts of Healing. This healing ability, given supernaturally by the Holy Spirit, is leading and guiding individuals to operate under His power to bring about healing.
>
> Prayers for healings and miracles are so important. My ministry focuses on reaching hard-to-reach people and showing them the truth about Jesus. When we do big projects and crusades overseas, the healings and miracles get the attention of the Hindus, Buddhists, Muslims, agnostics, atheists, the religious tribals, animists, and those of any other spiritual belief system. They realize their gods, or idols of stone, wood or even precious metal, have not healed them. The healings and miracles from our prayers instantly get their attention and let them know that there is one true and living God, and the way of salvation is through His Son Jesus. These prayers bring people to Jesus.

All twenty of the ministry leaders I interviewed said they have routinely prayed for people for healing, and often many were healed. However, only five said they routinely operate in the Spiritual Gifts of Healing: Pastors Powell Lemons, John AD, David Paul, Waseem Yousaf, and Mr. Worldwide Evangelist. All of them conduct ministry predominately in countries outside of America. Apostle Naomi Dowdy reported when she worked as an evangelist missionary to the Marshall Islands, she routinely operated in the Spiritual Gifts of Healing. Later, as a senior pastor in Singapore, she continued to see healings, but not to the extent she did as a missionary evangelist.

For me, I primarily stand in the office of teacher, bringing an explanation of the Word of God to others in the USA and around the world. I teach leadership and management courses formed from the experience I gained though thirty years in the U.S. Air Force. Occasionally, the Spiritual Gifts of Healing flow through me, leading to healing in others for whom I pray. I believe the reason I have acquired this intermittent gift is due to the miraculous healing I received from pancreatic cancer, detailed in the introduction. I feel blessed when the Holy Spirit flows through me in this way. I have witnessed many healings while in areas of great need, especially where medical facilities were scarce and too expensive for those living in poverty.

During one overseas trip in 2014 to Kathmandu, Nepal, I was presenting the Gospel and praying for all individuals who came to see medical doctors through Hand of Hope. We had been at different locations throughout Kathmandu for a week, and through a translator, I always prayed individually for anyone who asked for it. I had prayed for several hundred people, but I did not see evidence of any immediate healings until our last day. A man who had lost his hearing many years prior came up for prayer. Nothing miraculous happened immediately, so I went on to pray for the next person. About ten minutes later the deaf man started running all around the tent, yelling at the top of his lungs: "La, la, la, la." I asked my translator to go see what was going on. The deaf man said his hearing had returned! He was overjoyed, and it was wonderful to see that man's hearing restored by the Lord.

Let's hear some stories about the power of the Spiritual Gifts of Healing from our ministry leaders:

> **Apostle Lana Heightley:** I have witnessed three individuals who routinely operated in the Spiritual Gifts of Healing, each to a different degree and focus. One year I was working in the Philippines with several local women pastors. After we finished our ministry service, we set up prayer lines so each of us would pray for the service attendees. There was a certain older local woman minister who had the Spiritual Gifts of Healing, and every person she prayed for was immediately healed. And, of course, people saw it, and everybody would leave our lines and go to her because she had that amazing healing gift from the Lord.
>
> Once, I worked with another woman who had the gift of healing heart problems. Whenever she prayed for someone with a heart issue, they would be healed. Also, my father had a unique gift for healing legs. Every person who had a leg issue, whether they were in a wheelchair

or they could not walk, would be immediately healed when my father prayed for them. It was a mystery, but I do think that there are different Spiritual Gifts of Healing, and those are a few examples.

Pastor Waseem Yousaf: The Holy Spirit often gives me a vision of people who have problems in certain parts of their bodies. This is another gift of the Holy Spirit, called the Gift of the Word of Knowledge, where I become aware of issues going on with people at that specific point and time. God shows me the body parts which need prayer and healing through a vision. Then, I get the message from the Lord that somebody needs healing in that part of their body. For example, if someone has the problem of stomach pains, God will show me an image of that body part through prayer. Having seen that vision of the specific body part, I would pray for that person for their healing, and they are often healed.

Mr. Worldwide Evangelist: I have seen certain individuals that were anointed to heal specific things. I knew one minister who had a focus for healing deaf ears. He could almost always get them open by the power of God.

I also have operated regularly in the Spiritual Gifts of Healing since I was quite young. I began operating in healing without even fully understanding the tie to great faith. I was still a youth in single digits when the Lord used me to heal my aunt at a Christmas function. She fell ill in a back room and called me to quickly lay hands on her. So, I just prayed a simple prayer for her. I did not feel any special power, nor did my words wax eloquent, but she was immediately healed and back up moving around. All symptoms were gone, and she was testifying to the whole family that God had raised me up to go forth and see mighty miracles, mighty healings.

When I was just starting at Oral Roberts University in my pursuit of my bachelor's degree, probably around eighteen years old, God started using me to flow in healing without any major spiritual message being preached. One day in my dorm, a fellow student had fallen ill and was in the bathroom. I casually said, "Brian, be healed in Jesus' name." The founder of this university was a great healing evangelist, so I just said it kind of half joking, but half serious. Just a few moments later he

> came to my room and told me every symptom had left him, and he was completely healed.
>
> So, throughout my lifetime, I have seen God just heal people. I believe that gift became evident because of seeing it in my younger years, even without much teaching nor having a strong biblical foundation. I knew God wanted to heal, but I did not understand all the dynamics of healings. I had not preached a message on healing nor miracles. I really believe it revealed early on that I was going to be flowing in his Gifts of Healing. I am so grateful that God, by His grace and goodness, allows me, a mortal man, to flow in His power in such a way. It is one of the highest honors ever.

In summary, like the Apostle Paul said in 1 Corinthians 12, we should eagerly desire the spiritual gifts, especially the Spiritual Gifts of Healing. If you hear that someone is sick and you immediately want to pray for them, that is the Holy Spirit prompting you. It is often a sign that the Lord desires you to continue to pray for others, and the Spiritual Gifts of Healing are stirring inside of you. You can ask the Lord to entrust you with the Spiritual Gifts of Healing, but remember that frequently the Holy Spirit gifts can come and go.

Chapter 7

HOW WERE PEOPLE HEALED IN THE BIBLE?

GOD REVEALED HIS POWER BY HEALING PEOPLE MULTIPLE DIFFERENT ways in the Bible. There is a distinction between the Old and New Testaments in who God healed and how he brought about healing.

What Does the Bible Say About This Question?

Numbers 21:8: "The LORD said to Moses, 'Make a snake and put it up on a pole; anyone who is bitten can *look at it* and live.'" (emphasis added)

2 Kings 5:14: "So he went down and *dipped himself in the Jordan seven times*, as the man of God had told him, and his flesh was restored and became clean like that of a young boy." (emphasis added)

Matthew 8:14-15: "When Jesus came into Peter's house, he saw Peter's mother-in-law lying in bed with a fever. *He touched her hand* and the fever left her, and she got up and began to wait on him." (emphasis added)

Matthew 12:9-10a, 13: "Going on from that place, he [Jesus] went into their synagogue, and a man with a shriveled hand was there. . . . Then *he said to the man, 'Stretch out your hand.'* So he stretched it out and it was completely restored, just as sound as the other." (emphasis added)

Mark 7:32-35: "There some people brought to him a man who was deaf and could hardly talk, and they begged Jesus to place his hand on him. After he took him aside, away from the crowd, Jesus *put his fingers into the man's ears*. Then *he spit and touched the man's tongue*. He looked up to heaven and with a deep sigh said to him, '*Ephphatha!*' (which means 'Be opened!'). At this, the man's ears were opened, his tongue was loosened and he began to speak plainly." (emphasis added)

John 21:25: "Jesus did many other things as well. If every one of them were written down, I suppose that even the whole world would not have room for the books that would be written."

Acts 5:15-16: "As a result, people brought the sick into the streets and laid them on beds and mats so that at least *Peter's shadow might fall on some of them as he passed by*. Crowds gathered also from the towns around Jerusalem, bringing their sick and those tormented by impure spirits, and all of them were healed." (emphasis added)

Acts 19:11-12: "God did extraordinary miracles through Paul, so that even *handkerchiefs and aprons that had touched him were taken to the sick*, and their illnesses were cured and the evil spirits left them." (emphasis added)

Let's Look Deeper:

The verses above are just a small example of the varied ways people were healed in the Bible. Sometimes the healings were quick, but at times God specified actions to be done first before the healing arrived. Ed Melick, in his book *Healing Plunge*, did a great study of all the different healings throughout the Bible, determining 343 passages of Scripture concerned healing, including 108 accounts of supernatural healing.[1] Not every healing account lists how the healing came about, but we can track the many unique ways healing occurred.

Let's review the main ways healings were conducted during the Old Testament and the New Testament, with a focus both on how Jesus healed in the Gospels and the work of His disciples after the resurrection.

1. Old Testament Healings

There are some unique characteristics of the healings in the Old Testament. They always showed God's power and usually held spiritual or symbolic significance. Old Testament healings were holistic, in that they were more than physical healings and included forgiving sins, transforming people's hearts, and bringing them back into relationship with God. These healings were tied into the covenant established between God and His people. This meant there were blessings for people when they followed God's commands and consequences when the people sinned and were disobedient to God. When His people were disobedient, the Lord often directed them to conduct a specific task to receive their healing. For example, in Numbers 21:4-9, after the Israelites committed great sins against the Lord, poisonous vipers were released and attacked the people. Moses asked for healing for the people, and God directed him to make a pole with a bronze snake on it. The people only had to look upon the pole with the bronze snake to be healed (Numbers 21:8). The symbol of the snake on the pole is still used in the medical community today.

Prophets were sometimes used to either bring healing or deliver a message from God for healing. The Prophet Elisha sent a message to the military commander Naaman, who had leprosy. After hearing how he needed to be healed, Naaman had to swallow his pride and be obedient to do exactly what the Lord directed through Elisha. Once he dipped into the Jordan River seven times, he was healed (2 Kings 5:14).

The combination of prayer and faith to obtain healing was common throughout the Old Testament. King Hezekiah's prayer in Isaiah 38:15-20 resulted in the healing of his terrible illness and fifteen more years of life. In Genesis, we find three examples of prayer with corresponding faith for women who were barren and unable to have children. Abraham prayed for and, eventually in God's timing, received a son through his wife Sarah, as did Isaac for his childless wife, Rebekah. Rachel, the favorite wife of Jacob, also became pregnant only after seeking the Lord. In 1 Samuel 1:10-11, only though fervent prayer did Hannah become pregnant and bear the Prophet Samuel.

2. New Testament Healings

Jesus brought healing to a new level in the New Testament, emphasizing faith and including the Holy Spirit. Not only did Jesus demonstrate God's power, but as His Son, Jesus introduced new ways of healing as a large part of His ministry. Most of Jesus' healings were accomplished in different ways, in a very public setting, and included healing to more than just the Jewish people.

Instead of the emphasis on prayer found in the Old Testament, the two biggest actions facilitating healing in the New Testament are "spoken words or commands" and "touch." The book *Healing Plunge* documented that "spoken words" were used by the largest margin (twenty-seven occurrences), and "touch" by the second highest (twenty-two times). The remaining twenty-nine occurrences of healing were brought about in twelve different ways. Healing through "spoken words" typically occurred as a bold command by the healer. The verses in the beginning of this chapter show a few other ways of healing, including through spitting, the belief of being touched by Peter's shadow, and the dispersing of items touched by the healer.

Jesus' healing was selfless and humble. He did not command people to follow Him before He healed them. He demanded no loyalties or payments and expected nothing in return. No one was "unworthy" of healing to Jesus. His focus was to demonstrate God's love to all people and, in that, to relieve them of their pain and suffering. He did this by touching people or speaking commands of healing over them (Matthew 8:14-15 and Matthew 12:9-10a, 13). He even touched lepers, which no one else did in that time. In some cases, Jesus gave a person a specific action to perform, and only when they stepped out in obedience and faith to complete that action were they healed.

Jesus also opened the door for healing and ministry to non-Jewish individuals. Jesus said in Matthew 15:24, "I was sent only to the lost sheep of Israel." But He went on to heal a Canaanite woman's daughter and a Roman centurion's servant, and spent several days with the Samaritans (story found in John 4:4-42).

When studying the Gospels, we see that people frequently came to Jesus with the faith to be healed. Nowhere in the Bible did Jesus refuse to heal someone who came to Him with the faith for healing. On a few occasions, a person's faith was so strong that when they came to Jesus, only a touch or a word from Him would result in healing.

It is fascinating that Jesus used spitting three times in the act of healing (see story in Mark 7:32-35). Back then, much like today, spitting at someone was a sign of contempt. But Jesus used it for healing to challenge those negative perceptions and transform them into blessings. Some scholars think it was Jesus' way of showing deep compassion by touching someone with His own saliva. Some even believe that when Jesus, "spit on the ground, made some mud with the saliva, and put it on the man's eyes," (John 9:6), this was a reference to God's creation of Adam out of the dust of the ground, showing the power and authority of Jesus over creation. Early Roman and Jewish writings connect saliva with medicinal properties, so Jesus may have used it to signal healing. Thankfully the Lord has not asked me to spit on someone as a means for healing, as I know it would not go over well in most places. However, the more we are obedient to the Lord as we pray, the more He will use us as His vessels to heal others.

We know Jesus' ministry was vast and involved a great deal of healing. John, who was with Jesus throughout His ministry, wrote that books could not contain all the works He did during His short time on earth (John 21:25).

Healing did not end after Jesus left the earth and joined His Father in heaven. Jesus was very clear that He gave the same power and authority to His disciples, and all those who believed in Him. All the apostles continued the work Jesus started, sharing the Gospel and humbly healing others.

The Apostle Simon Peter became the leader of Jesus' followers after His resurrection. They had received some power and authority from Jesus to heal every disease and sickness and drive out impure spirits in His name (Matthew 10:1; this was addressed in chapter 4). In Acts 2:2-4, the Holy Spirit came upon the disciples at Pentecost, and even more power and authority were given to them. Shortly after this, Peter came across a lame beggar at the temple gate. Peter simply said, "Silver or gold I do not have, but what I do have I give you. In the name of Jesus Christ of Nazareth, walk" (Act 3:6). Instantly the man's feet and ankles became strong, and he jumped up to his feet. These healings continued: "The apostles performed many signs and wonders among the people" (Acts 5:12a). Many people had such confidence in the apostles and Christ's presence in their work, they believed even Peter's shadow would heal them as he walked past. (Acts 5:15-16). The Bible doesn't claim people were healed that way but showed the high levels of their faith and expectations for miracles through Jesus' apostles. All who came to them were healed.

The later chapters of Acts primarily detail the journeys of the Apostle

Paul, who had a strong healing ministry. Paul, originally known as Saul, was initially an enemy of followers of Christ (this story is found in Acts 8:1-3), until Jesus appeared to him on the road to Damascus. A bright light caused him to fall to the ground, and he temporarily lost his sight. Then Jesus appeared to Paul and asked him why he was persecuting His followers. This resulted in Paul's salvation and his commitment to follow Christ (this story is found in 9:1-31). Paul was then sent by the Lord to spread the Good News of the Gospel to the Gentiles, and eventually he wrote most of the New Testament. Paul was primarily an evangelist, missionary, and teacher of the Word of God. Wonders and miracles were common in Paul's ministry, which included a great deal of healing. This was evident when people were healed by handkerchiefs and aprons that Paul had touched (Acts 19:11-12). Paul's numerous miracles involving healing and protection also include the survival of himself and an entire ship after a shipwreck, being bit by a poisonous snake without effect, and healing the father of the chief official while stranded on an island.

It is exciting to know God moves and heals in so many different ways. Remember that signs, wonders, miracles, and healing continued long after Jesus departed the earth. Jesus' healing power and authority were passed to His followers, and that includes all of us today. When we have faith to know the Lord will heal and will use us as His vessels to bring about healing, we only need to be obedient when the Lord has us pray for others. We cannot "mess up" someone's healing by doing it the "wrong" way. Use the actions of Jesus as a model; be selfless, humble, pray for all people, and consider all worthy of healing.

Chapter 8

CAN WE RECEIVE HEALING FOR OUR SPIRIT?

YES, WE CAN RECEIVE HEALING FOR OUR SPIRIT; THE SPIRIT IS SEPARATE from our soul and body, but is equally important.

If our spirit becomes troubled or wounded, it is because our standing with God is not right. Our spirit can be healed by restoring our relationship with the Lord.

Unbelievers do not have an activated spirit of God, so they are not in communion with the Holy Spirit.

What Does the Bible Say About This Question?

I Thessalonians 5:23b: "May your whole spirit, soul and body be kept blameless at the coming of our Lord Jesus Christ."

John 4:24: "God is spirit, and his worshipers must worship in the Spirit and in truth."

I Corinthians 2:11-13: "For who knows a person's thoughts except their own spirit within them? In the same way no one knows the thoughts of God except the Spirit of God. What we have received is not the spirit of the world, but the Spirit who is from God, so that we may understand what God has freely given us. This is what we speak, not in words taught us by human wisdom but in words taught by the Spirit, explaining spiritual realities with Spirit-taught words."

John 14:26: "But the Advocate, the Holy Spirit, whom the Father will send in my name, will teach you all things and will remind you of everything I have said to you."

Jude 20-21: "But you, dear friends, by building yourselves up in your most holy faith and praying in the Holy Spirit, keep yourselves in God's love as you wait for the mercy of our Lord Jesus Christ to bring you to eternal life."

I Corinthians 14:14-15: "For if I pray in a tongue, my spirit prays, but my mind is unfruitful. So what shall I do? I will pray with my spirit, but I will also pray with my understanding; I will sing with my spirit, but I will also sing with my understanding."

John 14:16-17: "And I will ask the Father, and he will give you another advocate to help you and be with you forever—the Spirit of truth [the Holy Spirit]. The world cannot accept him, because it neither sees him nor knows him. But you know him, for he lives with you and will be in you."

I Corinthians 2:14: "The person without the Spirit does not accept the things that come from the Spirit of God but considers them foolishness, and cannot understand them because they are discerned only through the Spirit."

Let's Look Deeper:

In reviewing 1 Thessalonians 5:23, we see the Lord created us with three parts: a spirit, a soul, and a physical body. Our soul includes the mind, will, and emotions. Our spirit helps keep control over our soul, which then keeps our body pure and submitted back to God.

1. What is our spirit, and why is it important?

In the Bible, our human spirit is described as a vital but non-physical part of all of us, which connects us to God and enables spiritual life. It's a fundamental part of our being that is oriented to God, but it is separate from our soul and our body. Most people don't understand that everyone has a spirit. However, only believers have an active spirit which is in communion with the Holy Spirit.

> **Apostle Lana Heightley:** We are dead to spiritual things until we accept Jesus as our Savior. Once we accept Jesus, it activates the spirit within us and ties our spirit with God's Holy Spirit.

Our spirit is important since it is how God communicates with us. The Holy Spirit can reveal God's thoughts and desires to us in our spirit. When believers focus their thoughts on God and His Word, they will gain a greater understanding of His ways and discover how to be more like Him and less like the world. Jesus told us about God and how we should worship Him in the Spirit and in truth in John 4:24. God is spirit and soul, and Jesus was as well, until He came to earth in bodily form to reveal His Father to us. The verses in 1 Corinthians 2:11-13 tell us that only our spirit understands our thoughts, and in a similar way, only God's Spirit understands what He is thinking.

To fully understand what God desires for us, we need to become familiar with the voice of the Holy Spirit. He speaks to believers in many ways, and it is different for each person. For me, I hear from the Holy Spirit anytime I intentionally give Him the time and space to speak into my life. It is usually through the quiet journaling I do every morning, followed by reading the Word of God, then praying in my spiritual prayer language until I hear in my heart the message the Holy Spirit has for me. The Holy Spirit wants to teach us, guide us, and reveal things from God to us; we just have to give Him the opportunity to speak to us.

We see in John 14:26 that Jesus promised the Holy Spirit would come. Then God delivered the Holy Spirit to all believers in Acts 2:1-13. The Holy Spirit is in us, and He will guide us when we trust in Him and listen to Him. Jesus said we will receive power when the Holy Spirit comes upon us. This power transforms us into more effective witnesses as we share the Gospel at home and around the world.

2. How do we heal our spirit when it has been wounded?

When our spirit is not anchored to the Holy Spirit, it is troubled and needs healing. Healing only comes from restoring our spiritual relationship with God.

Licensed Professional Counselor Brenda Rogers tells us about some excellent techniques for helping to heal the spirit:

Spiritual woundedness at its core centers on our relationship with God. We need spiritual healing when our relationship with Christ or his body, the church, is wounded. When our difficult emotions, thoughts, and behaviors are oriented toward grievances about God or his body, the church, it is likely that we need spiritual healing. Our spiritual practices and the prayers of others can bring healing to our spiritual woundedness. When we pray for spiritual healing for another person, the Word of God spoken out loud over them has the power to act as a healing balm to their spirit. The Word of God can miraculously open our heart to receive the healing love of God and his church. When we read Scripture silently or aloud, it activates the process of spiritual healing in us. Other spiritual practices such as engaging in worship, praying in the Spirit, practicing Christian meditation, and gratitude journaling can also act to usher in our spiritual healing. When we struggle with a resistance to spiritual practices, we may seek out and/or unexpectedly encounter the healing love of God through walking outside in nature, interacting with animals or children, or engaging in a hobby that touches our spirit with the love of God. Our aim in spiritual healing is that our hope in Christ, the meaning and purpose of our lives, and our will to live life fully are reignited and restored amid a renewed intimacy with God and his body.[1]

3. How do we keep our spirit healthy?

To keep our spirit healthy, we should stay in a close relationship with the Lord through His Word, fellowship with other believers, and prayer. Our relationship with the Lord needs appropriate upkeep and attention, just like any other relationship in our lives. We cannot maintain a healthy and thriving relationship with our spouse or kids if we only spend one hour with them on Sunday mornings, and the same goes for our relationship with the Lord. We should try to spend time with the Lord every day and keep our spirit in constant contact with the Holy Spirit. I believe one of the best ways to do that is by speaking in tongues, or your prayer language.

The Gift of Tongues first came at Pentecost and is described in Acts 2:1-13. Paul also wrote about the gift of tongues in 1 Corinthians 12:1-12, 27-31 and 14:1-40. It is a gift for all believers from the Holy Spirit, where you speak out loud in a language that is not your own. It is your spirit speaking directly to the Holy Spirit. You can receive this gift by praying and asking the Lord or having a Spirit-filled believer pray with you. We see in Jude 20-21 how praying in the Holy Spirit builds us up in God's love. Paul confirmed that in 1 Corinthians 14:4a: "Anyone who speaks in a tongue edifies themselves." It brings power, guidance, and healing to our spirit, and strengthens us from within. Paul also referenced this in 1 Corinthians 14:14-15, explaining that when we pray or sing with the spirit, we achieve a new level of understanding as our spirit syncs with the Holy Spirit. Paul prayed in the Spirit a great deal: "I thank God that I speak in tongues more than all of you" (1 Corinthians 14:18). The benefits of speaking in tongues include increasing the power of your prayers and adding guidance and healing to your spirit, so that it may better control your soul. Paul told us to "pray continually," (1 Thessalonians 5:17) and I interpret this to mean praying in tongues almost constantly throughout the day, to keep our spirit tied in with the Holy Spirit. During those times when we don't know how to pray for a person or situation, praying in tongues can help. It is our pure spirit crying out to the Holy Spirit to find the right words that contain God's will for the affected person.

4. Do unbelievers have a good understanding of God?
No! Worldly people and unbelievers can never fully understand God nor the Holy Spirit. Jesus first spoke about this in John 14:16-17, when He said the Holy Spirit will come, but the world will not be able see or understand Him. The Holy Spirit communicates directly to believers, but unbelievers do not have an activated spirit in the same way believers do. Paul emphasized in 1 Corinthians 2:14 that an unbeliever cannot really understand God's works or the Holy Spirit, as both are seen as "foolishness" to them.

We should continue to pray for those who neither know nor understand God and the power of His Holy Spirit. Our prayers for unbelievers should focus on divine revelation in their lives, and for them to surrender to God's will in their lives. Jesus said in John 6:44a, "No one can come to me unless the Father who sent me draws them." With our dedicated prayers, the Holy Spirit can draw unbelievers to their Father God and open their hearts to the love of Jesus Christ.

In summary, healing for our spirit comes when we establish a healthy relationship with God through His Son Jesus. What joy to know our spirit is alive through the power of Holy Spirit. If we want to stay in alignment with God, our spirit must submit to the Holy Spirit and allow Him to guide and direct our lives. Once our spirit is tied to the Holy Spirit, we can keep our soul and body in line with God's Word. To keep our spirit healthy, we must stay in close contact with the Holy Spirit; one way to achieve this is by praying in tongues.

Chapter 9

CAN WE RECEIVE SOUL HEALING (WHICH INCLUDES EMOTIONAL HEALING)?

YES, OUR SOUL—WHICH INCLUDES OUR MIND, WILL, AND EMOTIONS—can receive healing.

Emotional healing is not talked about as much as physical healing, but it is equally or *more* important.

Attempting to heal emotional woundedness requires special considerations and comes with greater responsibility. Always refer to an appropriate professional counselor or psychiatrist when needed.

What Does the Bible Say About This Question?

Psalm 103:1: "Praise the Lord, my soul; all my inmost being, praise his holy name."

Revelation 6:9: "When he opened the fifth seal, I saw under the altar the souls of those who had been slain because of the word of God and the testimony they had maintained."

Psalm 6:3: "My soul is in deep anguish. How long, Lord, how long?"

2 Corinthians 4:4: "The god of this age [Satan] has blinded the minds of unbelievers, so that they cannot see the light of the gospel that displays the glory of Christ, who is the image of God."

Matthew 10:28: "Do not be afraid of those who kill the body but cannot kill the soul. Rather, be afraid of the One [Satan] who can destroy both soul and body in hell."

Romans 12:2a: "Do not conform to the pattern of this world, but be transformed by the renewing of your mind."

Matthew 26:38-39: "Then he said to them, 'My soul is overwhelmed with sorrow to the point of death. Stay here and keep watch with me.' Going a little farther, he fell with his face to the ground and prayed, 'My Father, if it is possible, may this cup be taken from me. Yet not as I will, but as you will.'"

Isaiah 33:2: "Lord, be gracious to us; we long for you. Be our strength every morning, our salvation in time of distress."

Ecclesiastes 3:1-8: "There is a time for everything, and a season for every activity under the heavens: a time to be born and a time to die, a time to plant and a time to uproot, a time to kill and a time to heal, a time to tear down and a time to build, a time to weep and a time to laugh, a time to mourn and a time to dance, a time to scatter stones and a time to gather them, a time to embrace and a time to refrain from embracing, a time to search and a time to give up, a time to keep and a time to throw away, a time to tear and a time to mend, a time to be silent and a time to speak, a time to love and a time to hate, a time for war and a time for peace."

Matthew 11:28-30: "Come to me, all you who are weary and burdened, and I will give you rest. Take my yoke upon you and learn from me, for I am gentle and humble in heart, and you will find rest for your souls. For my yoke is easy and my burden is light."

Let's Look Deeper:

1. Understanding our soul. What are our mind, will, and emotions? The soul is an important part of our makeup as humans and is mentioned almost one hundred times throughout the Bible. The soul is responsible for all our choices in life, so there is an ongoing battle within it. How do we choose between purity or sin, good or evil, peace or conflict? Often, real-life decisions are not so black-and-white. Before becoming believers, our soul tends to focus primarily on its own wants and desires. Once we become believers, our spirit can help our soul stay in line with the Holy Spirit and the Word of God. We see David praising the Lord with all his soul in Psalm 103:1. Then in Revelation 6:9, there is a reference to our souls in heaven. Our soul is what will face judgment when we die.

At times, our souls can be troubled. In Psalm 6:3, King David talked about his soul being in anguish, and he cried out to the Lord asking how long it would be that way. Even Jesus said, "My soul is troubled" (John 12:27), as He discussed what was coming in His future.

Although there is not a specific Bible verse that spells this out, most Bible scholars believe our soul consists of our mind, will, and emotions. Our mind is "what we think"; our will is "what we chose to do"; and our emotions are "what we feel." Let's briefly examine each area:

Mind: Thoughts in our mind run constantly. For many of us, we have a difficult time shutting off our thoughts. Our thinking tends to be the biggest battlefield with our enemy, Satan. Paul wrote in 2 Corinthians 4:4a that Satan "has blinded the minds of unbelievers, so that they cannot see the light of the gospel." Satan does his best to convince unbelievers that neither he nor God exists. Satan predominately operates in our minds, telling us we can "get away with" many different sins. Jesus gave us a stern warning in Matthew 10:28 to watch out for Satan, who can lead us to an everlasting hell. He is the devil on your shoulder whispering disruptive thoughts into your head. Learn to recognize this evil voice and order him to flee in the name of Jesus—and he will.

We can keep our mind "healthy" by keeping it focused on the things of God. Paul wrote in Romans 12:2 that as believers we should not focus on the world but keep our mind renewed. We can keep our mind renewed through prayer, studying the Word of God, and having fellowship with other believers. Paul also wrote in Philippians 4:7: "The peace of God, which transcends all understanding, will guard your hearts and your minds in Christ Jesus." Paul also reminded believers that we have the mind of Christ already—so we only need to walk in faith and keep our mind focused on Christ and not the world.

Will: Our will is the second part of our soul. The Lord has given us all free will, but His desire is for us to follow His will as laid out in the Bible.

Satan is always trying to tempt us into sin, but it's our will that makes the decision: to follow Satan or follow the Lord. I understand not every choice is clear cut, and there can be some gray areas. If it's not clear, stay in prayer until you hear from the Lord, or talk with other trusted believers to help guide you when facing difficult decisions or choices.

To keep our will "healthy" we should keep it in line with the Word of God. Right before Jesus was arrested, He went to the Garden of Gethsemane to pray. He knew His immediate future held terrible physical pain and emotional betrayal. He told His disciples, "My soul is overwhelmed with sorrow to the point of death" (Matthew 26:38a). But then Jesus surrendered to His father and said in the next verse, "Yet not as I will, but as you will." As believers, we should keep our will surrendered to God's will.

Emotions: The third part that makes up our soul is our emotional state. All of us feel a great range of emotions on any given day, and even Jesus is described in the Gospels as experiencing the full range of human emotions: grief and sorrow (John 11:35), compassion (Matthew 14:14), anger at religious leaders (Mark 3:5), and even anger at His own disciples (Mark 8:33). However, emotional wounds from trauma can impact the soul and disrupt our peace. Let's journey deeper into the ways to identify emotional turmoil and how to heal this part of the soul.

2. How can we work through emotional healing?

We can work through emotional healing with the Lord alone, but usually it is helpful to work with others on this journey. This type of healing is greatly needed today for both believers and unbelievers, so be sensitive and willing to pray for others for emotional healing, along with physical healing.

When we define emotional pain, this can manifest as a variety of conditions, including depression, anxiety, anger problems, substance use disorder, or any combination of these and more. Emotional pain can sometimes have stronger effects on the body than physical pain, or it can even manifest in the body as physical complaints. Most people face trauma and/or internal struggles in their lives. Some are dealing with it actively, and some have residual emotional wounds from trauma they faced early in their lives. Sometimes, they do not even recall the events but can still deeply feel the pain of abuse, rejection, betrayal, and sin.

Even Isaiah asked God for help managing internal distress during difficult times (Isaiah 33:2). An internal struggle is much harder for people to talk about than a physical struggle, and sometimes people may not even be aware of their own emotional turmoil and its impact on their life. Despite this, God our Great Physician is committed to healing our broken hearts and making us whole. The Bible verses referenced in this chapter show us that emotions are recognized by God and are an important part of our lives. There are so many seasons we endure throughout our lifetime, as shown in Ecclesiastes 3:1-8: times of death, times of healing, times of weeping and laughing, times of mourning and dancing. Regardless of what we are going through, Jesus wants us to know we can turn our problems over to Him, and in Matthew 11:28-30 He promised to give "rest for your souls."

As believers, we can and should pray for emotional healing when it is needed. But we always need to remember that prayer ministry or altar ministry is not a counseling session. All believers are not automatically skilled mental health counselors, so it is better to refer someone to seek a mental health professional when needed. If you are regularly praying for people, you should have a list of local professionals you can refer others to. If your church does not have counselors on staff, ask for a list of recommended professionals that can be distributed to those in need.

There are occasions when the Lord may bring miraculous and quick emotional healing. However, usually these wounds are healed slowly and progressively over time. When praying for people with emotional trauma, it is important to remember that it is easy to cause them *more* harm, even when trying to help. Asking someone to tell you the traumatic event that happened to them often causes regression and worsening of their condition; it can bring uncontrollable emotions and flashbacks to the forefront of their mind, which they have not yet learned to deal with safely. Licensed professionals undergo extensive training to work with patients who have severe trauma, including post-traumatic stress disorder. These conditions require step-by-step processes, including trauma-informed care practices and cognitive behavioral therapy. The Word of God does not speak against the use of doctors and medicines to bring about emotional healing, so they should be recommended when needed. People need to work through these hurts, with the Lord and others guiding them along the way.

Licensed Professional Counselor Brenda Rogers provides some

important information that all of us should be aware of when praying for others needing emotional healing:[1]

> Most theories about emotions agree that emotion is a human response to a personally significant stimulus, which results in a biological and a psychological reaction. Emotions are beneficial to us in that they alert us and can help guide our behavior toward positive life outcomes. We may experience the basic emotions of sadness, happiness, fear, anger, surprise, and disgust, as well as more complex emotions such as love, embarrassment, envy, gratitude, guilt, pride, or worry.
>
> Sometimes troubles and losses in life can cause us to experience difficult emotions. The experience of difficult emotions does not necessarily mean that we need emotional healing. What we may need in the face of troubles and suffering is emotional comfort, not emotional healing. We can provide emotional comfort to others through specific prayers, quiet presence, and practical deeds. Most often, we simply need someone to sit with us in our pain and suffering, without platitudes, without efforts to bring cheer, and without easy fixes. It is healthy for a person to allow these difficult emotions to be fully experienced.
>
> Emotional woundedness occurs when our emotions are not leading us to grow in Christlike thinking and behavior about ourselves and others. When our difficult emotions, thoughts, or behaviors are oriented toward grievances about ourselves or others, it is likely that we need emotional healing. Because our emotional woundedness most often occurs in unhealthy relationships, it is most powerfully healed through loving and healthy relationships with others. We can pray for broken relationships with self or others to be restored through hope, repentance, forgiveness, wisdom, and love in the context of healthy relationships.
>
> Emotional woundedness can result in extreme emotional distress based on our life circumstances and genetic predisposition. When we recognize severe distress in another, we can pray for their emotional healing and the support they may need. We can lovingly offer them resources for more specialized spiritual care or mental health care. When a person is so distressed that they want to hurt themselves or others, we are responsible to assure that they access the emergency mental health care that they need.
>
> Emotional pain is often the result of a negative relationship, or a

difficult experience which has been interpreted by the individual into emotional pain. These painful emotions are most often grief, shame, loss, guilt, betrayal, abandonment, and rejection. All of us have suffered through these emotions at one time or another. These painful emotions then transfer to painful thoughts about the events, circumstances, the other person, and even against God. These thoughts can further progress to a physical pain in our bodies, through stress or even physical ailments due to the emotional pain. All this can lead to a painful spirit within us, as we question our faith, the church, and our relationship with God.

What do people need to process emotional pain and gain emotional healing:

1. Presence: Others to sit with the person in their pain and suffering (silent presence).
2. Expressed Empathy: "I am sorry. / It sounds so difficult. / I can't imagine."
3. No Platitudes: No "time heals, just forgive"/ no cheering up / no taking sides.
4. Acceptance: Permission to be where the person is / "It's okay to be where you are."
5. No Judgment: Free to have their own perspective and response / "No judgment about this."
6. Companionship: Be with the person in their daily life / "You're not alone; I'm with you."
7. Acts of Service: Ask about needs, extend basic care (drop off meals, do laundry, etc.).
8. Impart Hope: Offer to share small acts of enjoyment (walks, music, play, etc.).[1]

For a list of specific prayer points for emotional healing, go to chapter 20.

Let's hear from some of our ministry leaders concerning emotional healing:

> **Pastor David Paul:** Comforting others is the key to inner healing. I really enjoy working through inner healing and leading someone into real breakthrough from the inside out. It is sometimes a very long process, and you need to invest the time to walk with them through it. It takes

> a good understanding of the Word of God and walking people through the Word. But, when you see that person being transformed by love, by the Holy Spirit, of course, and by the Word of God, it is amazing and a true victory.
>
> **Pastor Walt Landers:** I have seen a significant increase in the need for emotional healing in my network of churches. We need to be more conscious about this season where church attendees are struggling much more mentally and emotionally, more than ever before. Recently, one of our campus pastors preached on emotional healing. Then, he did an open invitation for prayer at the end of the service and was shocked when most of the congregation came forward for mental and emotional healing.
>
> **Superintendent Aaron Hlavin:** I witnessed my wife go through an emotional healing journey. After serving the Lord in her youth, she drifted away in college, until a friend's drunk driving accident brought her back to the Lord. At church the following night, the Lord spoke directly to her, like He was washing her emotions like an old-fashioned scrubbing washboard. God did something in her life and spirit. From that night, God began to do emotional healing in her in a big way. She and her mom always had a complicated relationship, but a few years later, God reminded Jamie of that altar moment and said, "You need to have an emotional scrubbing with your mom." So, Jamie started to build a new relationship with her mom. They both worked at it and had four years of incredible relational growth. Then her mom got cancer and died seven years later. Jamie said God had done a lot in her life, but one of the best emotional healings was the Lord showing her she needed to fix her relationship with her mom before she got sick. Then, Jamie knew it was a true relationship, not just reestablished because her mom was dying. My wife was healed of her emotional trauma by trusting in the Lord and doing what He told her to do.

Like most of you, I've had several deep emotional wounds over the years. Often, I would only remember the ugly, angry, and bitter words or actions of others, and I could not let go of the emotional pain it caused me. I struggled with holding grudges for long periods of time without forgiveness. I would relive situations repeatedly, thinking of ways I could have handled the situation better, stood my ground, or fought back. One of the best things I did for my emotional pain was to go through the eight-week Cleansing Stream Seminar in 2003, hosted by my local church in Colorado Springs. Not only did that seminar focus my spirit and soul on the Lord, but it significantly helped my emotional healing. During the final weekend retreat, I remember a session where we released and let go of all the people who had hurt us in our past. Our task was to write down the names of all the people who hurt us on small slips of paper. Then I went to a prayer partner, and we prayed individually over each name. I first prayed for the person who hurt me, then spoke the words to forgive them, and then as my prayer partner would pray over me, I would tear up that slip of paper and let it drop to the ground, releasing that person to God. I did that for every person, and afterward I felt such a release. I forgave them, released them to God, and let it go. It was a great emotional healing experience for me, and I strongly recommend the seminar to others who thrive in structured settings and prefer fellowship groups around them for support.

Remember, our soul is a vital part of our internal makeup, and we should not underestimate the prevalence of emotional distress or the importance of emotional healing. Emotional pain is just as real as physical pain, and though we should feel empowered to pray for healing in this area of great need, we need to exercise additional caution. It is our responsibility to refer to a mental health professional when needed, and to ensure that anyone at risk of harming themselves or others get immediate help from an emergency department or crisis center.

Chapter 10

HOW ARE OUR BODIES HEALED TODAY?

Our body is temporary and a part of us only while we are here on earth.

There are four ways our bodies can be healed, and there is a time factor that goes with each healing. Superintendent Hlavin says, "For every believer, we are guaranteed to be healed either medically, progressively, or miraculously, and when we are disappointed it does not happen on earth, we are healed eternally."

What Does the Bible Say About This Question?

Genesis 2:7: "Then the Lord God formed a man from the dust of the ground and breathed into his nostrils the breath of life, and the man became a living being."

Romans 12:1: "Therefore, I urge you, brothers and sisters, in view of God's mercy, to offer your bodies as a living sacrifice, holy and pleasing to God—this is your true and proper worship."

Matthew 9:12: "Jesus said, 'It is not the healthy who need a doctor, but the sick.'"

Luke 17:14: "When he saw them, he said, 'Go, show yourselves to the priests.' And as they went, they were cleansed."

Mark 1:41b-42: "He [Jesus] said, 'Be clean!' Immediately the leprosy left him and he was cleansed."

Philippians 3:20-21: "But our citizenship is in heaven. And we eagerly await a Savior from there, the Lord Jesus Christ, who, by the power that enables him to bring everything under his control, will transform our lowly bodies so that they will be like his glorious body."

Revelation 21:3-4: "And I heard a loud voice from the throne saying, 'Look! God's dwelling place is now among the people, and he will dwell with them. They will be his people, and God himself will be with them and be their God. "He will wipe every tear from their eyes. There will be no more death" or mourning or crying or pain, for the old order of things has passed away.'"

Let's Look Deeper:

Our bodies were made from the dust of the ground (Genesis 2:7), and that is where they will return. When Peter wrote in 2 Peter 1:13, "as long as I live in the tent of this body," he was reminding us that our body is a temporary, easily damaged structure, not something permanent. Paul wrote in Romans 12:1, we should never sin with our body but offer it as a "living sacrifice" to God. Our soul controls our body, to keep it in line with the Word of God.

Superintendent Hlavin breaks down the ways that the Lord can bring about healing into four broad categories: medically, progressively, miraculously, and eternally. We will go in depth about each of these below.

1. Medicine is a means for physical healing.

Whether a believer or an unbeliever, we know medicine heals people. Every year, new medical ways for healing are discovered, whether through advancements in medical knowledge, new techniques for surgical procedures, or novel prescription medications. Some medical healings will be quick, but others may take an extended period. All of us should stay under the care of a primary doctor for routine and preventative care for our bodies.

People were never condemned by Jesus for visiting doctors. Jesus even made a comment that it was the sick who need a doctor (Matthew 9:12). Today, the Lord makes doctors and medicines available to us, and advances in technology continually provide new ways and means for healing.

One of the reasons I chose the Assemblies of God to be credentialed as an ordained minister was their foundation of beliefs. They believe in God's divine healing; however, they also state the "divine healing neither opposes nor competes with medical doctors."[1] In my personal healing story told in the introduction, I believe I was miraculously healed from pancreatic cancer. However, the nine-hour Whipple surgery was still medically necessary to remove the tumor to prevent recurrence, and it took my body weeks to heal internally. As I age in this life, I routinely seek advice and care from medical doctors.

> **Superintendent Aaron Hlavin:** God has created medicine to be able to help us, and God created doctors to know how to use their skills to assist in the healing process. There are doctors in the Bible, even evidence of them using medical procedures in Biblical times.

2. Our bodies heal progressively.

Generally, progressive healing occurs over a longer period of time, whether it be physical or emotional. Even divine healing can manifest in stages, with incremental improvements rather than a complete and immediate healing. Progressive healing is more common in individuals with chronic illness. Sometimes it is not a complete cure, but to receive enough healing to improve quality of life or make the pain tolerable.

> **Superintendent Aaron Hlavin:** God has made our bodies to heal progressively. When you cut your hand, your body knows how to heal the cut. So, there is a natural progression that God's created within our bodies.

> **Pastor Sabrina Chow:** Some healing takes time; it may not be immediate, but it can be the next day, the next month or few months, or years of progressive healing. So just press in to pray and not give up.

> **Pastor Lisa Chin:** One of my favorite verses to pray with people is Psalm 41:3, which says, "The LORD sustains them on their sickbed and restores them from their bed of illness." It gives them hope during their progressive recovery time. Healing can be instantaneous but can also occur over time.

Jeremiah wrote that the Lord declared, "I will restore you to health and heal your wounds" (Jeremiah 30:17a). This verse implies a process of recovery. Another verse that shows healing as a process rather than instantaneous is Luke 17:14. In this story, ten lepers approached Jesus and asked for healing. They were not healed right away, but as they traveled to show themselves to the priest. We do not know how long of a walk they had to see the priest, maybe several hours to several days.

I have had several orthopedic surgeries, including fixing wrist fractures, meniscus tears, and a total knee replacement. I was healed in all the surgeries, though not instantaneously. They all required time for my body to fully complete the healing process. When praying for others going through difficult illnesses or surgeries, remember that sometimes healing appropriately requires hard work, including lengthy and painful physical therapy sessions that may last for months. This long and arduous process is often the only way to return to good functionality and decrease chronic pain, so praying specifically for strong motivation, strength, and perseverance can be helpful.

3. Miraculous healing still happens today.

All the ministry leaders I interviewed for this book have witnessed some sort of miraculous healing. In the Bible, there are many examples of miraculous healings, like the one listed in Mark 1:41-42, where the leper was instantly healed by Jesus.

During one of my mission trips to the Philippines, our group traveled to many different villages throughout the island of Mindanao. We would do skits to attract the people in the villages, and people would come up to each of us for prayers after our presentations. On one occasion, I was praying with a teenage girl who had a huge mass on her neck. It stuck out at least three inches and was the size of a softball. She said it developed when she was young and continued to get bigger every year, and it was starting to affect her swallowing. The people in her village told her she was cursed. Normally, I have people put their own hand on the affected area when we pray, but she would not touch it due to fear. So, I put my hand on it and started to pray over her. As I prayed and declared God's healing power, I felt the mass shrink down to nothing; she was completely and miraculously healed. Praise the Lord! I was so humbled the Lord used me to bring His healing power.

The Lord often uses this type of healing today in evangelistic crusades. I have witnessed many healings during these crusades in the Philippines and throughout Pakistan. As I mentioned previously, evangelists often operate in the Spiritual Gifts of Healing to facilitate these healings to show the power to God to unbelievers. This type of miraculous healing seems to predominately happen in areas of the world hungry for the Gospel and in people who have the faith to believe healing and miracles will occur.

4. Eternal healing is for all believers.

If neither medical, progressive, nor miraculous healing happens on earth, then it will happen for all believers in heaven. Our bodies are temporary and do not go with us when we die. In Philippians 3:20-21, we see our bodies will be transformed into spiritual, glorious bodies. This is a beautiful end-of-life story for all those who are believers and followers of Jesus Christ. We see in Revelation 21:3-4 how wonderful it will be for the righteous to go to God's dwelling place when they die, to a place without "death or mourning or crying or pain."

> **Superintendent Aaron Hlavin:** All believers will be healed eternally of all things when they get to heaven. We can take comfort in knowing our final healing will take place there, and we will no longer be in pain or suffering. This should encourage us to do everything in our power to make sure all others go there with us, regardless if they are friends, family, or our enemies.

When I witnessed my mom's suffering during her pancreatic cancer battle, I prayed fervently that healing would come, but it never did. I held my mom close and was reading Psalm 23 over and over to her in her final moments as she passed away. I was greatly comforted knowing she went into the arms of Jesus in heaven and was eternally healed.

In summary, we focused on four different types of healing that can occur in our bodies. The Lord may use medicine and doctors to help us heal. Healing may occur progressively over a period of time, or in some cases, we may see miraculous, instantaneous healing. We can know for sure, as a believer, that we will feel no more pain or distress in heaven. Our final healing will occur eternally, once we are in heaven dancing on the streets of gold with Jesus.

Part II:

WHAT ARE THE ANSWERS TO DIFFICULT HEALING QUESTIONS?

Chapter II
WHY ISN'T EVERYONE HEALED?

We cannot explain why some people are healed and others are not. We know God is sovereign, and He operates according to His will and in His timing.

Behaviors and attitudes such as unforgiveness, bitterness, doubt, and unbelief can hinder healing.

Some people identify strongly with their sickness or disability, so they find it difficult to accept or allow healing. However, also be careful not to label people as disabled or in need of healing when they may not be.

What Does the Bible Say About This Question?

John 5:2-9a: "Now there is in Jerusalem near the Sheep Gate a pool, which in Aramaic is called Bethesda and which is surrounded by five covered colonnades. Here a great number of disabled people used to lie-the blind, the lame, the paralyzed. One who was there had been an invalid for thirty-eight years. When Jesus saw him lying there and learned that he had been in this condition for a long time, he asked him, 'Do you want to get well?' 'Sir,' the invalid replied, 'I have no one to help me into the pool when the water is stirred. While I am trying to get in, someone else goes down ahead of me.' Then Jesus said to him, 'Get up! Pick up your mat and walk.' At once the man was cured; he picked up his mat and walked."

Matthew 6:15: "But if you do not forgive others their sins, your Father will not forgive your sins."

Ephesians 4:31: "Get rid of all bitterness, rage and anger, brawling and slander, along with every form of malice."

Hebrews 3:19: "So we see that they were not able to enter, because of their unbelief."

Deuteronomy 29:29: "The secret things belong to the Lord our God, but the things revealed belong to us and to our children forever, that we may follow all the words of this law."

Luke 13:10-13: "On a Sabbath Jesus was teaching in one of the synagogues, and a woman was there who had been crippled by a spirit for eighteen years. She was bent over and could not straighten up at all. When Jesus saw her, he called her forward and said to her, 'Woman, you are set free from your infirmity.' Then he put his hands on her, and immediately she straightened up and praised God.'"

Mark 8:22-25: "They came to Bethsaida, and some people brought a blind man and begged Jesus to touch him. He took the blind man by the hand and led him outside the village. When he had spit on the man's eyes and put his hands on him, Jesus asked, 'Do you see anything?' He looked up and said, 'I see people; they look like trees walking around.' Once more Jesus put his hands on the man's eyes. Then his eyes were opened, his sight was restored, and he saw everything clearly."

Let's Look Deeper:

We don't know all the reasons why some people are healed and others are not. We know God is sovereign and all things happen according to His will. In the story in John 5:2-9, Jesus healed one lame man by the Bethesda pool, but He didn't heal any of the others who were there. No biblical explanation is given.

I don't know why I survived pancreatic cancer while many do not. About five years after my recovery, a coworker was diagnosed with pancreatic cancer. He and his wife were strong Christians, and my miraculous healing gave them hope. However, when he didn't survive his cancer battle, his wife became very angry. She asked me, "Why were *you* healed but not my husband?" She was grieving, and I didn't have an answer other than he was healed eternally. We cannot pretend to know God's reasoning; although it is difficult, we should do our best not to dwell on things we will never understand. What we do know is that God is capable, God is able, and we should trust His sovereignty and His will.

Sometimes we do not give God credit for the healing and miracles He does in our lives. To most people, my dad was disabled. His left knee was surgically fused together when he was very young due to a severe injury and subsequent infection. He was in the hospital for seven years, from age five to twelve, at a time before antibiotics were used in medicine, and he was unable to bend the knee for the rest of his life. My dad was an incredible man who never felt limited by his knee; he worked for forty years as an iron worker, working suspended on bridges and walking on steel construction beams many stories high. The only thing my dad could never do was pedal a bike.

My parents were practicing Missouri Synod Lutherans, and I remember my parents taking my sister and me to a "healing service" at the civic center in downtown Saginaw, Michigan. It was the mid-1970s, and my dad went on stage to meet with the "healer" to see if his knee would be healed so he could bend it, but nothing happened. I don't know anything about this healer—if he was authentic, Spirit-filled, or a fraud, and I don't know the degree of my dad's faith in his own healing. However, many years later, my dad met with a physician at the Mayo Clinic who told him his recovery and current functionality were indeed miraculous. Usually, when young children have a joint fused before they finish growing, the leg has stunted growth or grows abnormally. My dad was told that most people who had that procedure spent their life on crutches, or with a deformed shorter leg. God did perform a miracle for my dad; he gave him unprecedented healing in the form of exceptional functionality. During those long years in the hospital and through the prayers of his mother, he was given a normal life.

Many of the ministry leaders quoted unforgiveness, bitterness, and unbelief as reasons some people are not healed. Let us briefly define each of these:

Unforgiveness: According to Dr. Michael A. Milton, the state of holding onto resentment toward someone who has wronged you, refusing to release them from the perceived debt of their offense. This can negatively affect a person's mental health, leading to increased stress, anxiety, and even depression.[1] See Matthew 6:15.

Bitterness: "Anger and disappointment at being treated unfairly."[2] "In the Bible, bitterness is not merely a fleeting negative emotion, but a deep-seated, festering resentment and anger that can negatively impact a person's spiritual life and relationships. It is often the result of unresolved hurts, unfair treatment, or unmet expectations, and can lead to a hardened heart and defiled relationships."[3] See Ephesians 4:31.

Unbelief: "Lack of religious belief or absence of faith."[4] In the Bible, unbelief is a refusal to believe in God, His Word, and His promises. It's not just intellectual doubt, but a willful rejection of faith. It is often portrayed as a serious sin with negative consequences, both in this life and the next."[5] See Hebrews 3:19.

We should stay vigilant to not let any of these three invade our lives. God commands us to love one another (Leviticus 19:18), and Jesus tells us in Luke 6:27-28, "But to you who are listening I say: Love your enemies, do good to those who hate you, bless those who curse you, pray for those who mistreat you."

Let's review how several of the ministry leaders answered this question of "Why isn't everyone healed?"

> **Apostle Les Bowling:** We need to start by understanding Deuteronomy 29:29. Some things God will reveal to us, but there are secret things that belong to the Lord. If someone doesn't get healed, I just leave it in God's hands. We just need to keep praying for people and trusting God. We need to listen to the Holy Spirit, because there could be bitterness or unforgiveness that needs to be resolved. Sometimes those things can be barriers, but not all the time. If the Holy Spirit prompts me in that way, then I will, with grace and discretion, try to administer correction to that person. However, I never want anyone to go away feeling shamed or not worthy to be healed.
>
> It's difficult to bring healing to some people, like hypochondriacs who are always sick. Their glass is always half empty, or there has never been water in their glass. They tend to be very negative, with the attitude of "Woe is me; I'm always sick, I'm going to be sick tomorrow." Their identity gets tied to their sickness, and that's where they get attention and empathy. Maybe they are lacking in an emotional area of their life

where they need empathy and want attention, but it's the wrong way to get it. These mindsets can even follow family lines, as some people believe they have the same sickness passed down from other family members. If that person wants healing, they must be willing to let go of the sickness. If I'm walking in the right kind of healing anointing, healing will happen, but only if I can make them let go of it. I remind them of the promises in God's Word, and what Christ still does for us today. We celebrate instantaneous gifts of miracles, but at times healing is more of a restorative process. We must remember there is no cookie-cutter thing that works for everybody. Everybody's context, circumstance, and journey are different.

Director Jill Boyonas: I believe God has the best plan for a person's healing. We may think God's way is hard if there is any suffering. If immediate healing doesn't happen, we need to trust that God has other plans. The most difficult thing for people to accept is the timing for them to go home to be with the Lord. I remember what the famous preacher Kathryn Kuhlman said on her deathbed. Some pastors came to offer prayer, but she said, "I'm going home to be with the Lord." Because the truth is, flesh and blood cannot inhabit God's final kingdom; a person must die to get to heaven, unless we are still alive when Jesus returns. So healing is just temporary. Even raising the dead is temporary. But the world should know that the God who we are serving is alive and powerful.

Pastor Lisa Chin: I believe sickness and illness are actually because of the Fall of Man, and its consequences. It is the decay of the human body. Those who are sick need to repent of their personal sin but as the same time, we should not condemn every person who is sick, blaming every sickness on sin. Once we confess and repent, we are forgiven. We do not need to repent hundreds of times for our healing. For example, if someone had cancer, was healed, and lived a good life for many years, but the cancer came back, does it mean the person's sins were not forgiven? No. I think people need to be very clear; it is the frailty of the body. People should not be judged and condemned that every ailment is because of their sin. A person's specific sickness is not always a direct consequence of their personal sin. People need the faith to believe in divine healing from God.

Pastor Sabrina Chow: Here are the reasons people do not receive their healing:
1. The will of God. For example: their time is up on this earth, and they have finished their race, so God takes them home.
2. Sin of unforgiveness resulting in bitterness. I have seen illnesses from this, as some have certain stomach ulcers, aches, and pains.
3. No repentance of sin, which causes the sickness. For example: drinking alcohol causing liver cirrhosis, smoking causing lung and throat cancer, addictive gaming causing insomnia, a promiscuous lifestyle causing venereal diseases.
4. No repentance of generational curses. They have inherited demons from their ancestors due to curses and vows made by their ancestors.
5. No change in lifestyle to live healthily. They do not take care of their "tent." No exercise, lack of sleep, living a stressful lifestyle, eating unhealthily.

Missionary Jared Dietrich: We should never make an excuse or try to explain the reason why someone isn't healed. Most of the time, we don't have a clear explanation when people are not healed. Sometimes I will pray again a second or third time. We hope to have a success rate like Jesus one day, but we are all growing in Him. I believe very much that Jesus always desires to heal–in His way and in His timing.

Apostle Naomi Dowdy: Throughout my seventy-plus years doing ministry, the greatest hindrance to a believer receiving healing is unbelief. They may have hope for healing, but they don't have faith for healing. Hope is something we look to in the future, but faith is an action verb, especially as it's written in James 5:15. Another hindrance is people believing they're not worthy of God healing them. These are some of the things that can block healing.

Apostle Lana Heightley: We all love it when we witness miraculous, instantaneous healing, but healing can come slowly as well. I've seen people depart from our healing meetings and come back the next day, saying, "Right after I left here, God opened my ear, and I can hear." I don't take responsibility for people not being healed, since Jesus does the healing; I just believe that God can and will. So, just keep praying and believing for healing.

Superintendent Aaron Hlavin: I will use myself as an example. I have a genetic muscle disorder that I haven't been healed from yet, even though many have prayed for me. When I'm under a lot of stress, I will have an outbreak, which at times will take a couple weeks for me to recover. The doctors do genetic tests and tell me I have a genetic flaw, but I still believe in the possibility of God's healing. I tell people, "You didn't get the healing you needed today, so just hold on to the possibility of healing in the future," which keeps God in the right spot. He is still God, so it's still possible. If someone says, "I've been prayed for ten times," well, what if it happens on the eleventh time? It can just happen without prayer, maybe when you are driving down the road in your car. I don't know when God is going to heal, but just believe it will happen. I try to be honest with people and tell them, "I wasn't healed yet, so I'm in the same boat as you, believing that healing will come in God's timing." So, I steer people to staying hopeful and in faith for healing.

We also need to accept those situations when someone doesn't want or desire healing. For example, I had a blind guy who wanted to attend my church. He said, "I'm not going to come to your church if people are only interested in seeing me healed from my blindness. I don't want to be healed. I've been blind my whole life. At sixty-three, this is my life; I'm comfortable with it, and I don't have any desire to see now. It would scare me to be healed this late in life. I want my first time to see to be when I'm in heaven." So, I assured him that he could refuse any prayers he didn't want over his life.

Pastor Walt Landers: We need to ensure we don't allow blessing blockers, such as bitterness, unforgiveness, and offense, into our lives. I knew of a woman in Texas, Mrs. Dodie Osteen, who was diagnosed with terminal liver cancer in 1981. As she prayed and declared healing scriptures, she realized she had some offense, some unforgiveness, and there had been some broken relationships. The Lord brought her to this place of restoration, and she wrote letter after letter asking for forgiveness from everyone the Lord suggested. She was quickly healed of her cancer and survived many more years. She wrote a book about her journey, "Healed of Cancer" in 2017. She just passed away from natural causes at ninety-one years old in July 2025. So, there are some things that can block healing from freely flowing into our lives.

We should all think about our own blessing blockers. The Bible tells us in Proverbs 4:23, "Above all else, guard your heart, for everything you do flows from it." This means to keep our hearts from harboring unforgiveness, offense, and bitterness. I have seen really bitter people struggle with a lot of health issues. It's important to let those issues go and give them to God. I've had to let go of bitterness when some close friends were very disloyal. It's not easy, but it's a lot better for my life not to be in a place of unforgiveness. If I'm doing anything that is short-circuiting the anointing or the Word of God in my life, I want to get it corrected quickly. Proverbs 17:22a tells us, "A cheerful heart is good medicine."

Pastor Powell Lemons: The main thing I've seen that has limited healing in people is sin in their lives. There are many Scripture verses that correlate sin with sickness. But remember, Jesus mentioned that for the man born blind in John 9:1-3, it was not due to any sin in him or his parents. So, we must be very careful about that.

Missionary Mary: I expect healing, and I've experienced a lot of healing. So, if I do not see somebody healed, I usually suspect there's some sort of spiritual stronghold, or something deeper is going on. For example, many times I've prayed through a line of people, and every single person in that prayer line received instant healing, no matter what their sickness or problem. Suddenly, when the last person receives prayer, nothing seems to happen. It's unusual. Then, I find out they just arrived and missed the Gospel presentation. God tells me to stop the healing prayer, so they can get their life right with God first. It's not that a person must be a Christian to receive healing, but that God wants to ensure they hear the Gospel. In other cases, there was demonic oppression that needed to be dealt with before they received healing. There have been other times when someone didn't receive immediate healing, and I'd pray a second time like Jesus did in Mark 8:22-25. *If Jesus can pray a second time, I can too.* Sometimes it takes persistence in prayer or contending for healing with a person, standing in faith with them for healing. Sometimes it takes weeks, months, and even years. Jesus said some people didn't receive healing because of their unbelief. So, I must be sure that my faith is partnering with God. I don't pass judgment on the other person, but there's always the possibility that person is not standing in faith for their own healing.

Pastor David Paul: I've had many experiences of healing not coming when I pray with people. When it happens, the enemy usually brings discouragement, so we speak the Word of God over people, and they get encouraged to trust in God's promises for healing. When some receive instantaneous pain relief, though not complete healing, we keep believing that full healing will come soon. *I always remind people to have faith in Jesus, the one who heals, not the person who is praying for them.* Sometimes the people in Sri Lanka get too focused on the person who is praying for them, especially if it's a minister from another country. So that lack of faith in God is always a challenge here. Another problem is those who sadly take pride in their sickness. Last year, an elderly lady visited my church, and she told me, "Well, I have been sick now for thirty years," like it was an achievement. I said, "Should I congratulate you for being sick for thirty years?" So, I had to correct her, to remind her to never say such a thing. She needed to see her identity in Jesus and not in her sickness.

I've also had to correct people against using negative words over someone's sickness. A mother and her daughter started coming to my church, and the first thing the mother said was, "My daughter has epilepsy." She would say this to everyone all the time, and then complain about her daughter's epilepsy. Sadly, the daughter felt very insecure. So, I told them both to stop highlighting the sickness, and I trained them to speak by faith in healing and wholeness through the Lord. After that, the daughter had less epilepsy symptoms, and she is now completely healed.

Pastor Jim Westheim: I believe there are reasons people do not receive healing. Some don't believe that it can happen, but I believe God can heal despite that. Some sickness is just part of life, and other times sickness is under death. Both kinds can bring glory to God if that person allows God to do that. Sadly, when some believers get sick, they spin out of control and question their faith. If they don't see immediate healing, they become bitter and angry with God and walk away from Him. We need to do our best to help people facing that situation.

Mr. Worldwide Evangelist: In my ministry experience, the main reason people don't receive healing is their unbelief. Unbelief will shut down healing almost every time. When people think or say, "I doubt you or God can do this, or I don't believe in healing," it will not come. Even if you're operating in a powerful godly manifestation, you cannot overturn someone's will if they will not be open to healing. A minister friend of mine, who operated often in the Gifts of Healing through the Holy Spirit, told me a sad story about a lady in a wheelchair who was wheeled forward by her husband for healing prayer. As the minister was praying, the power of the Holy Spirit came so strongly upon them, she literally was lifted out of the chair and was feeling her legs being completely made whole. But then, she grabbed the wheelchair and yanked herself back down, saying, "Bless God, but I'm going to die in this wheelchair." And she did. The power was present to heal that lady; she could take steps, but she chose not to receive. God will not override someone's will to choose. Unbelief, even in the ministry of Jesus, is recorded as a stalemate to the power of God flowing. The Bible says in Matthew 13:58 that Jesus could not perform many mighty works in His hometown of Nazareth, because of their unbelief. He said a prophet is going to be without honor in his own home area where people are too familiar: "Oh, that was just Joseph and Mary's kid. I saw Him grow up. Surely, He can't heal me." And that doubt and unbelief limited Jesus. "And He was not able to do even one work of power there, except that He laid His hands on a few sickly people [and] cured them" (Mark 6:5 ampc). Unbelief is the greatest stopper and stalemate of the power of God. So we teach people the Word of God, and if they will just keep listening and learning, and healing will come. But, if they are determined to doubt and have unbelief, there's not much that we can do.

In summary, there are several reasons people don't acquire their perceived healing. Maybe the healing will come in God's timing, or maybe there are things in their lives, like lack of faith, bitterness, or unforgiveness, that will block healing. Sometimes, people identify strongly with their illness, so they have difficulty accepting healing; other times people may not actually need the healing we think they do. At times, the frailty of the body prevails, and we must accept that it is time for someone to leave the earth and go to heaven to be with Jesus. Whatever the case, we should ask the Holy Spirit for discernment when praying with others and accept that we will never fully understand the patterns of God's healing.

Pastor Hibroon Khokhar gives us great closing words:

Regardless of if we see immediate healing or not, we still need to thank God, praise His name, and believe He will do it at the right time.

Chapter 12

CAN PEOPLE LOSE THEIR HEALING?

THERE IS NO CLEAR BIBLICAL GUIDANCE ABOUT WHETHER PEOPLE LOSE their healing, so there is a wide range of viewpoints. However, many agree that certain behaviors and lifestyle choices can affect and dissipate healing.

What Does the Bible Say About This Question?

Luke 17:12-19: "As he was going into a village, ten men who had leprosy met him. They stood at a distance and called out in a loud voice, 'Jesus, Master, have pity on us!' When he saw them, he said, 'Go, show yourselves to the priests.' And as they went, they were cleansed. One of them, when he saw he was healed, came back, praising God in a loud voice. He threw himself at Jesus' feet and thanked him—and he was a Samaritan. Jesus asked, 'Were not all ten cleansed? Where are the other nine? Has no one returned to give praise to God except this foreigner?' Then he said to him, 'Rise and go; your faith has made you well.'"

James 1:6-8: "But when you ask, you must believe and not doubt, because the one who doubts is like a wave of the sea, blown and tossed by the wind. That person should not expect to receive anything from the Lord. Such a person is double-minded and unstable in all they do."

Let's Look Deeper:

Of all the questions in this book, this one doesn't have a firm yes or no answer. I have never lost any healing I received from the Lord. However,

I believe Satan is good at convincing people either they were never healed or they are not worthy enough to keep their healing. When I interviewed the ministry leaders, this question had the most diverse range of answers. Let's review these different viewpoints about whether or not people can lose their healing:

> **Pastor Waseem Yousaf**: Yes, people can lose their healing for certain reasons. For example, if they are not thankful, obedient, and following Christ, they will lose healing. Only one out of the ten lepers came back to Jesus and was thankful for the healing of their leprosy (Luke 17:17). I have some doubts about the other nine lepers who did not thank Jesus, that maybe they did not receive a wholeness in their bodies. I believe if we don't testify Jesus and we don't have complete faith in Him, we can lose healings. If we don't stop sinning and turn away from wicked ways, we can lose healing. Once after Jesus healed a person, He told him, "Sin no more, that nothing worse may happen to you" (John 5:14, ESV).
>
> **Pastor Jim Westheim**: I don't believe people can lose their healing, as I have never seen that happen. I don't believe God is fickle. He does not give a gift, then take it away, whether it is a gift of the Spirit or a gift of healing. He heals because He wants to heal. He is a good God, and that does not feel good to me at all.
>
> **Mr. Worldwide Evangelist**: Absolutely, people can lose their healing. People can give up their healing by doubting they're healed. If our will is involved, and it's part of fighting the good fight of faith, we must contend for which God's provided for us. Paul said, by the Holy Spirit, to "fight the good fight of the faith" (1 Timothy 6:12). A good fight is a fight you win in faith, by not doubting in your healing.
>
> Sin is also a factor. There are lifestyles that will invite the darkness of the devil back into people's lives and cause problems. So, if someone chooses, after receiving the blessing of healing, to live a sinful life, their body will be affected by that sin. So, whether you're talking about evil spirits or sickness, there are things we can do to keep filled with the power of the Holy Spirit, so these things of the enemy will not affect us. The Bible says to, "Submit yourselves, then, to God. Resist the devil, and he will flee from you" (James 4:7), but we must be submitted to God

first. That's how the power of God flows, not the other way around. We cannot be out doing all the devil's junk and expect to be free of the devil's devices. To stand against the devil, we must be submitted to God in our lives.

There are also some people who don't trust God to provide for them when they are healed from a disability or illness that generates income. I've seen some walk away from their healing when they realize it will affect their income. Many years ago, as we were doing healing ministry in Peru, we approached this older woman who was a blind beggar on a street corner. She wore this string around her neck that held this little collection can for the money people gave to her. We prayed for her, and she was immediately healed, and she happily tossed away the can with joy. Her eyes opened, and she was very excited she could see. But as quick as the miracle came, by her own choice she lost it. Sadly, out of fear and angst, she ran over and grabbed that can, and when she did, she was lost trying to find her way again. She let go of her healing and lost her sight again, wondering, *How am I going to have a way to make money?*

Pastor David Paul: I've seen people who do not have the faith to hold onto their healing. A problem in Sri Lanka is people tend to believe what others say, instead of trusting in the Lord. People will get healed, but when others start to question it, or don't believe it happened, their doubts cause them to lose their healing. Just like in James 1:6-8, we cannot doubt the Lord or His miracles in our lives, and when we doubt, healing is lost to us.

Missionary Mary: I have experienced pain in the form of a reoccurring infection. It was healed, but then the pain came back. I don't know why it came back but I continued to pray for it and contended to receive permanent healing. Other believers also prayed and believed in faith with me and I was eventually healed and the infection never returned.

Pastor Powell Lemons: I don't see a Scripture pattern where it says you can lose your healing. However, we know Jesus said on one occasion, "Stop sinning or something worse may happen to you" (John 5:14). There might be another explanation. From what I have seen, when people return to the same lifestyle, the same sickness tends to return. For example, I have done a great deal of ministry in the Philippines, which is a large rice-producing country. Those that live or work in the rice-growing regions are routinely exposed to harmful smoke from burning the rice straw and stubble. I've seen many healed from the chest and lung conditions from the smoke, yet they return to the areas where the burning is going on, and their medical problems return as well.

Pastor Walt Landers: There are people who get healed and get sick again. The reasons can be environmental issues, lack of discipline, or lack of obedience. I wouldn't say they lost their healing, but they were healed and got sick again. I don't think you lose something that God gives you. We also need to ensure people do not allow the enemy or other people to talk them out of their healing. People need to remain strong in their confession that "they are healed."

Pastor Hibroon Khokhar: Yes, they can lose their healing. If they forget God and His presence, then they open the door for Satan to attack them. If they are not in the presence of God, protection is not guaranteed.

Apostle Lana Heightley: I don't see a biblical example of somebody being healed and then losing their healing. So, I'm not sure I believe that people can lose their healing, but I know that when we are healed, we need to be thankful. When Jesus healed the ten lepers and only one came back and thanked him, who knows what happened to the others. I think when God heals, He heals. However, returning to a harmful diet or lifestyle after being healed can bring about a return of the same problems.

Evangelist Tanveer Gill: I have seen bitterness and an unforgiving spirit impact healing. I have seen many healed by the miracles of God. However, I have seen people who, even after healing, keep a bitterness in their spirit, and they lose their healing. After any healing, people need to be thankful and increase their prayers and their time in the Word of God to keep their spirit whole and healthy.

Apostle Naomi Dowdy: Sadly, I've seen it happen. I remember a young man who was talked out of his healing. He was born with a limited hearing ability, and he had a device to help him hear. I talked with him about healing, prayed for him, and his hearing was completely restored. He left his hearing device for me to pass on to someone who needed it. Then two weeks later, he called me and asked for it back. When I asked why, he said, "My mother told me my healing cannot be real, since I haven't been able to hear since I was a baby." She kept telling him, "You cannot hear," and he believed her, and he lost his hearing again. So, people can talk you out of your healing; you have got to stand strong and believe.

Director Jill Boyonas: I have seen people lose their healing through lack of faith in God. We were praying for a lady in our village in Cebu in the Philippines. She had a lump on her breast, so I prayed for her. She started crying as the pain went away, and I knew she was healed. But later, when the pain came back, she went to a witch doctor. After a few weeks she died. So, some people can lose their healing because they do not trust God amid their pain. We need to keep our confidence steadfast till the end as we fight the good fight to receive our healing.

Apostle Les Bowling: I believe healing is only lost by people's choices, not by God. Christ is not only my message of ministry, but my model for ministry. When Christ healed people, they were really healed; there's not an account of them losing it. So, I ponder, *If they lost it, did they really receive it to begin with? Did they really get healing or just get released?* I don't know. I think if God provided the healing, it was only lost by that person's choice. Proverbs 18:21a says, "The tongue has the power of life and death." So, people can, through negative confession and constant negative words, talk themselves right back into sickness. Another problem is lifestyle choices. For instance, I knew a lady who was an avid smoker for many years, so cancer came in her body. Then, she was supernaturally healed, confirmed by the doctors, but she did not quit her lifestyle of smoking. Sadly, she kept smoking, and cancer returned. You think people would stop destructive behaviors when they are healed, but sometimes they don't.

> **Pastor John AD**: People can lose their healing and the power they received from God. I tell my church, "Once you plug the charger into the switch, it will keep charging. Once you take it out, the power is gone." We have seen people get healed and many possessed people set free. But if they do not stay in the Word, and do not stay in the presence of God, these demons attack them again. Once you are healed, you must stay close to the Lord and take time for Him. It is very important, because God is giving us a new life.

What a great range of viewpoints. Most believe God would not take away someone's healing, but people's lifestyles, choices, and destructive behavior to their bodies can cause a return of the same problems. Whenever I pray with someone for healing, I always give them a small card that has on it several healing verses from the Bible. I tell them to pick out a verse that speaks to them, then write out that verse and post it somewhere they see every day, like their bathroom mirror or fridge. Then, proclaim that healing verse and its promise over their life and stay in faith for God's healing. This helps to keep people from letting either themselves, their friends, or the enemy talk them out of their healing. It is also a good idea to remind someone healed of a disability from which they receive income that although it may be difficult to make a new life for oneself, they should trust that God can provide for them financially.

Chapter 13

IS THERE HEALING FROM A HARMFUL LIFESTYLE?

YES, WE HAVE LEARNED GOD CAN AND WILL HEAL ANYTHING. However, choosing to do harmful activities will result in consequences in our bodies.

The Lord can free people from their addictions, as well as the negative effects of those addictions. However, people must still resist temptation.

What Does the Bible Say About This Question?

1 Corinthians 15:33-34: "Do not be misled: 'Bad company corrupts good character.' Come back to your senses as you ought, and stop sinning; for there are some who are ignorant of God—I say this to your shame."

1 Corinthians 6:12: "'I have the right to do anything,' you say—but not everything is beneficial. 'I have the right to do anything'—but I will not be mastered by anything."

1 Corinthians 10:13: "No temptation has overtaken you except what is common to mankind. And God is faithful; he will not let you be tempted beyond what you can bear. But when you are tempted, he will also provide a way out so that you can endure it."

Proverbs 23:29-35: "Who has woe? Who has sorrow? Who has strife? Who has complaints? Who has needless bruises? Who has bloodshot eyes? Those who linger over wine, who go to sample bowls of mixed wine. Do not gaze at wine when it is red, when it sparkles in the cup, when it goes down smoothly! In the end it bites like a snake and poisons like a viper. Your eyes will see strange sights, and your mind will imagine confusing things. You will be like one sleeping on the high seas, lying on top of the rigging. 'They hit me,' you will say, 'but I'm not hurt! They beat me, but I don't feel it! When will I wake up so I can find another drink?'"

Galatians 5:1: "It is for freedom that Christ has set us free. Stand firm, then, and do not let yourselves be burdened again by a yoke of slavery."

1 Corinthians 6:9-10: "Do you not know that wrongdoers will not inherit the kingdom of God? Do not be deceived: Neither the sexually immoral nor idolaters nor adulterers nor men who have sex with men nor thieves nor the greedy nor drunkards nor slanderers nor swindlers will inherit the kingdom of God."

Psalm 34:17-18: "The LORD hears his people when they call to him for help. He rescues them from all their troubles. The LORD is close to the brokenhearted; he rescues those whose spirits are crushed." (NLT)

Let's Look Deeper:

Most of us have been tempted at some point to try things we know are harmful for our bodies. In today's world, drinking, smoking, and drugs are glamorized on TV, in movies, and on social media. Often, our friends and family members will put pressure on us to participate in harmful behaviors. Previous chapters taught us the importance of our body as a temple for the Lord. Living a life with excessive alcohol use, addiction to illegal or prescription drugs, smoking, disordered eating, and other activities that damage our bodies is not what God desires for us. Paul gave us a good warning in 1 Corinthians 15:33: "Bad company corrupts good character." I once had a coworker who was recovering from alcohol use disorder and an immature believer; he decided to go back to the bar scene to convince others not to drink. I sensed it was his will and not God's will leading this decision, so I warned him against it. Unfortunately, it didn't take long for him to revert back to a life controlled by alcohol and walk away from the Lord. In 1 Corinthians 6:12, Paul warned we have the right to do anything; however, not everything will be beneficial to us and our bodies. I applaud those who have the calling to minister to others by venturing back into potentially dangerous situations, but it takes strong spiritual maturity.

We all have different ways to cope with stress in our lives. Any activity can turn into a negative behavior if we take it to the extreme. For example, dieting can turn into binge eating, anorexia, or bulimia if not done in moderation. This is when we should turn to God, and others, to help us identify our true underlying problem that needs healing. Then, typically the goal is to attempt to transition to a healthy coping mechanism while fixing the underlying issues. *When we pray for others who are struggling, giving unconditional support is more important than judging the reasons for their actions and the effects of their lifestyle.*

We all are tempted by something, but there is good news written in 1 Corinthians 10:13. Everyone is tempted, but the Lord will never allow a temptation beyond what we can bear. I used to smoke cigarettes, and I still get tempted when I go to a gas station and see my old favorite cigarette brand in the display case. It was my older sister who got me into smoking in my teens, but I was never a regular smoker. As I got older, it became a stress releaser, even though I knew it was bad for my health. When I would get really stressed, I would hide out somewhere to binge smoke a pack or two, feel terrible, and quit again. Sometimes I would go without smoking for months, even years, but then I was always tempted to start again when I was stressed out.

In May 2003, I found out my husband was having an affair with a much younger woman, and it sent me into a destructive spiral of emotions and thoughts. My husband hated smoking, so in a weird way I felt I was getting back at him by smoking. I was sitting outside on my third straight pack of cigarettes when I strongly felt the Lord tell me to "put out that cigarette and throw the rest away." I was obedient, and then I committed to stop smoking. I've never smoked another cigarette, but that doesn't stop me from still being tempted. Despite their harmful effects, the physical sensation I received from them would help me stay calm when I struggled with my emotions on my own. Now I just remember what my Savior did on the cross for me and stand firm; He is all the strength I need to get me through uncontrollable emotions and thoughts.

Sadly, I watched my older sister struggle with an alcohol addiction from which she never broke free. She struggled with it her entire short forty-two-year life. She lived across the country from me, and every few years I would visit her and get her back into a rehab facility, which never lasted. As she came under hospice care for cirrhosis of her liver, I went once again to try to help her. She told me she loved and believed in Jesus and was once again done with alcohol. So, I ensured she received medical care and put her into another alcohol rehab facility. Later, I found out that the day she was released, she returned once again to her harmful lifestyle for "whatever" reason, bought another twelve-pack of beer, and died that night. When I read Proverbs 23:29-35, I grieve for how the effects of alcohol destroyed my sister.

There are other addictions that are less obvious but that can still harm us both physically and emotionally. These include gambling, video games/gaming, and even social media. Once, I spent a very frustrating ninety minutes stuck in a car with someone who I believe had a social media addiction. I rode with her to an event a few hours away, and after the event, she refused to leave the parking lot until she reviewed, edited, and posted all the photos she took during the event to her social media account. This type of addiction can be subtle, hard to identify, and tends to be accepted in modern society. Her actions impacted me negatively as a significant amount of my valuable time was commandeered by her, and she was unable to stop what she was doing so I could return home on time. An addiction is anything that controls *you*, instead of the other way around. When your actions begin to impact those around you negatively, it is time to self-reflect and see if an addiction is controlling your life.

I believe when someone is ready to be freed of their addiction, with faith and strong support, they can be healed in the name of Jesus. Galatians 5:1 gives us a great reminder that we are free in Christ and shouldn't allow ourselves to be put back under any yoke of sin. We are stewards of our body, and to purposely damage our bodies and then blame other factors is wrong. We shouldn't be surprised by the long-term consequences of our harmful life choices.

Our ministry leaders have provided outstanding and poignant comments on this issue:

> **Director Jill Boyonas**: Being delivered from smoking was the first thing I experienced as a new believer. An hour after I was saved, like usual I started smoking a cigarette, then violently threw up. No one told me

smoking was bad, so I tried again with my second cigarette, and I threw up again. From that moment on I was delivered from smoking and still have no appetite for it. A similar thing happened later that afternoon with alcohol. Every day after work, my friends and I would go to our favorite place and have a beer, or many beers. So, that afternoon we went to our bar, and as soon as I started drinking, I threw up again. Then, I realized something really happened to me when I was saved. In tears, I tracked down the woman who led me through the salvation prayer. She told me Jesus loved me enough to cleanse not only my heart but my body, His temple. I realized that emptiness in my heart left for good, and I fell in love with Jesus. So, I believe in deliverance from bad life choices, and we see this often in our crusades.

Pastor Lisa Chin: I have seen immediate release from addiction happen. After prayer, they just have a sudden distaste for smoking or excessive drinking. Then, it becomes a commitment of discipline, because they can still have the temptation to return to that lifestyle. Honestly, it happens rarely, but I pray it will happen more often. Some people choose to live a harmful lifestyle, whether it's excessive drinking, smoking, drugs, or even gambling. God can heal us from anything, but we need to be committed to change and trust God to help us along the way. It's really submitting your life to God and disciplining your lifestyle. It's a habit you must work through, and it may not be easy.

Pastor Sabrina Chow: Yes, God will heal all things, but it requires repentance and God's strength to overcome these addictions. I have heard of people who lose their desire to smoke and drink. For some, when they smoke, they feel like puking; for others, the desire for drinking is gone. I've heard of a few people who quit cold turkey to get rid of their drug addiction. God supernaturally delivered them by the power of the Holy Spirit.

Missionary Jared Dietrich: Yes, there is healing, but I also believe there are times the Lord leads us to make better lifestyle choices. I've known some people who were immediately delivered from a drug addiction and never had a temptation of a relapse again, while others had to go through a long detox and rehabilitation process to be free of their addiction. Why would God do that for one person and not the others? I don't know, but I believe God has His reasons.

Apostle Lana Heightley: I think there's healing, but first we need to take action to get rid of any harmful life habits. I have seen some people healed from the effects of smoking and excess drinking, but I have also seen believers suffer consequences from those activities in their bodies. This is a tough subject, as there has been a lot of conflicting guidance in biblical circles over the years. I've heard some church leaders say, "I'm not going to pray for any smoke-related healing for those people not willing to quit smoking." I don't take that kind of a stand, but I've told people, "I'm going pray those things make you sick," and I've seen it happen. Do I think a believer who smokes or drinks will go to hell? No. However, regardless of the excuses believers make to continue to do things that harm their bodies, they will eventually face physical consequences. It is all about being an "overcomer" and trusting in God to help you.

Superintendent Aaron Hlavin: Some people have instantaneous deliverance from addictions, and some do not. None of us will ever have that answer fully, outside of heaven. First, people need to really want freedom from their addictions. One of my church pastors was working with a guy who kept saying he wanted to get free from smoking, but then week after week, he would show up at church reeking of cigarette smoke. So, the pastor decided to be bold, and he asked the man to repeat this prayer to help him give up smoking: "I want to be freed from smoking more than anything in my life. I want to have my healthy life, so, Lord, the next time I take a drag on a cigarette, let me die." And the guy replied, "What? I'm not praying that!" While I don't suggest praying prayers like that, I do think we need to take our prayers seriously, asking God to help us overcome with great determination.

Pastor Hibroon Khokhar: With God's power, along with prayer and fasting, addictions can be overcome. Some people say with training and classes people can overcome drugs and addictions, but I have not seen any of my church people get healed from training centers. I have seen them overcome addictions when God gave them power to rebuke their addictions.

Pastor Walt Landers: We all eventually suffer the effects of our life choices. One time, a staff minister felt led by the Lord to meet with a couple from our church who were very, very unhealthy. This minister felt like he had a word from God that they needed to get checked out by a doctor. The husband said, "No, we're fine. We're happy; we eat whatever we want to eat and live however we want." Then, only a couple months later the young husband died and left his family in a bad situation. It was sad to realize this minister gave him a warning from God, but the husband would not listen, and his family suffered the consequences. So, let's live out our days in strength and health, and fulfill everything God is calling us to do.

We also need to honor God with our lives, especially if we have received healing. There was a young man in the ICU from battling the effects of a sinful lifestyle. I happened to be in the hospital when a friend of mine asked me to go pray for this young man with his family. The young man had already coded three times, and if he coded again, the family was not going to resuscitate him. My friend said, "This guy needs a miracle, or he won't live." So, I laid my hands on him, prayed over him, then walked out. A short time later, some of his family came to my church and told me that God completely healed that young man. Sadly, about a year and a half later, I ran into my friend, who told me that young man went right back into his old sinful lifestyle. One night while partying at a bar, he dropped dead on the dance floor. So, I think you must honor what God gives you and not mishandle it. That puts a little bit of the fear of God in all of us.

Missionary Mary: Yes! There are so many streams of healing. When we are praying for people who may have compromised their own body we can choose to pray with a heart of compassion rather than condemnation for the person we are praying for. Especially if they made poor choices that may have led to seemingly natural consequences. What are you going to do differently if the illness is from natural consequences versus spiritual consequences? Some people get lung cancer from other outside factors. Sometimes the person I'm praying for will say, "I have done this terrible thing, and I do not deserve healing." In all these cases, God's Word on healing is supreme above every other reasoning, and His forgiveness is complete. Any condemnation is not from God, so we need to be righteous in our actions. With these types of problems, we also need to remember the psychological wounds. It's not just healing for the physical issues, but the issues in their past and current situations which caused the addictive behaviors. When Jesus saw the crowds, He had compassion on them and healed all of their sicknesses. May we grow to see people the same way Jesus does.

Pastor David Paul: We need to focus on the person's inner healing first in these situations. I love ministering for deliverance from addiction and focusing on the inner healing more than the physical healing. Harmful life choices are often a result of being self-wounded. Whether you choose to be a drunkard, smoke, or do drugs, you do that because your inner being is hurt or wounded. When I seek the Lord on how to comfort and pray for these people, the Holy Spirit will often give me a word of knowledge or a revelation to the root cause of why they are doing what they are doing. I enjoy helping people work through inner healing and leading someone into real breakthrough from the inside out. Sometimes it is a long process. But when you see that person really being transformed by God's love, by the Holy Spirit, through the Word of God, it's an amazing victory.

Mr. Worldwide Evangelist: This covenant of healing that we have, which is part of the covenant of salvation, is never an excuse to go out and abuse the body. Look at what I Corinthians 6:9-10 says, that the unrighteous shall not inherit the kingdom of God. In other words, we should not willfully choose sin. We should be good stewards over our body and our mind, including our actions, thoughts, and deeds, since we are the temple of the Holy Spirit. Let's trust God and press in and see the good things that He has and wants to do on our behalf.

In summary, let's review two key Bible verses listed in the beginning of this chapter. Galatians 5:1 reminds us we have been set free from the slavery of sin, including all addiction; we just need to trust in Christ Jesus. Psalm 34:17-18 encourages us not to be afraid to call for help. I think the most powerful prayer we can ever pray is "Help me, Jesus!" He knows what is going on in our lives and is waiting for us to cry out to Him and surrender to His will. What a blessing to know the Lord is willing to rescue anyone who has the courage to ask Him for help.

Chapter 14

DOES GOD HEAL OLD-AGE AILMENTS?

Yes, God can heal anything, according to His will and timing. We just need to consider what is worthy of our time and focus.

What Does the Bible Say About This Question?
Isaiah 46:4: "Even to your old age and gray hairs I am he, I am he who will sustain you. I have made you and I will carry you; I will sustain you and I will rescue you."

2 Corinthians 4:16: "Therefore we do not lose heart. Though outwardly we are wasting away, yet inwardly we are being renewed day by day."

Deuteronomy 34:7: "Moses was a hundred and twenty years old when he died, yet his eyes were not weak nor his strength gone."

Psalm 103:2-5: "Praise the Lord, my soul, and forget not all his benefits—who forgives all your sins and heals all your diseases, who redeems your life from the pit and crowns you with love and compassion, who satisfies your desires with good things so that your youth is renewed like the eagle's."

Let's Look Deeper:
For years I have struggled with the question of whether God heals old-age ailments, so as I started this book journey, I was interested to see what the other ministry leaders thought about it.

From 2009 to 2011, I was stationed with the military in San Antonio, Texas, and attended a great church. The pastor had a strong healing gift; often he would call people to the altar, and many were healed. However, it bothered me when he would say, "Don't come up here for things like reading glasses and regular old-age aliments." I never knew his reasoning for saying this, but maybe it was as simple as not having the time to pray for everyone who had these more minor ailments. Regardless, I have always felt uncomfortable when anyone puts limits on what God can do for us. I believe God is big enough to heal anything when people come to him in faith.

As I get older, I have a few old-age ailments like arthritis, hearing loss, and the need for glasses. As I contend with an aging body, I still believe in healing or at least relief for my ailments. Have I asked God to heal my wrinkles or gray hair? No. But I do ask for healings in the areas that may limit my ability to do the work he has called me to do. Back in 2024, I had surgery to remove my cataracts, so I was medically healed, and now I am able to drive at night again. Even through my visual acuity didn't dramatically improve, thankfully my vision is still easily corrected with glasses. During a 2024 trip to Pakistan, Pastor John AD prayed over my hearing loss, and it has improved significantly since then. I still pray for healing for my arthritis, but I am also grateful for the pain medications, steroid shots, and the knee replacement that allow me to live a normal and active life.

As we all age and our frail bodies succumb to the issues of this world, we have great hope in Isaiah 46:4, knowing that God will sustain us and rescue us when needed. Also, 2 Corinthians 4:16 reminds us, even if our bodies are wasting away, we can and should renew our minds every day in the Word of God. The verses listed at the beginning of this chapter tell us God will sustain our youthful spirit and soul, despite the state of our bodies. As you will see many of the ministry leaders mention below, healing can happen for anything we have the faith to believe in, as long as it is within God's will and timing. However, we also need to accept, as the Bible says, that our bodies are "wasting away."

> **Pastor Waseem Yousaf**: Yes, God can heal old-age diseases. We see that often here in Pakistan, as God heals all kinds of sickness from our bodies.

Mr. Worldwide Evangelist: I believe there is healing for old-age issues. First, Moses is our example, as he was around well before salvation through Jesus in the New Covenant. In Deuteronomy 34:7, it highlights how Moses's eyes were not weak, nor his strength gone. Plus, he climbed the mountain God wanted him to climb to see the Promised Land before God took him and buried his bones. Why? Because Moses lived in the presence and the manifested power of God. I believe it transformed his body, so much so his face glowed with God's presence.

Now add the New Testament revelation of what Jesus has done in us, redeeming us from the curse of the law and putting His very Spirit inside us. If we have the faith to believe, our aches and pains will disappear. I believe we will hear when others have hearing aids. I believe we can see clearly without glasses. The biggest thing I want to emphasize is never to get condemned; just rise and claim what is yours. The famous preacher Smith Wigglesworth, from the early 1900s, had to work through kidney stones. He refused any surgery and was eventually healed. One of the things that I like to proclaim is, "Live long and strong," and I declare it over everyone I pray for.

Psalm 91:16 says, "With long life I will satisfy him and show him my salvation." Another good scripture is Psalm 103:2-5, which tells us of the many benefits when we praise the Lord: our sins are forgiven, we are healed from all our diseases, our life is redeemed, we are crowned with love and compassion, our desires are satisfied, and we are renewed like an eagle, even as we get older.

Pastor Jim Westheim: Yes, I've prayed for seniors in nursing homes and seen healing and relief from pain. Even my mom had severe arthritis as she entered hospice care, but she wasn't in any pain. But certainly, age has its limits. The Apostle Paul talked about his vision and his body failing. He recognized the fact that the human body was not meant to be eternal in its scope. Someday we will have a perfect spiritual body that God's prepared for us. So, we should just trust God as we walk through this life with some physical problems; it is just the nature of it.

Pastor Powell Lemons: Anything that's broken can be fixed by God. However, should we spend our time praying against reading glasses? I would say there are bigger health issues in my life that I'm wrestling with right now. As you get older, you start experiencing new things in your body, and everything starts working differently. Is it wrong to pray for old-age ailments? No, it's not wrong. Part of it is realizing our bodies are going to age.

Pastor Walt Landers: I'm at that place now as I'm in my sixties, and I've got some ailments here and there from old injuries. But I'm very much just believing that I'm going to stay healthy and finish my race strong with God's power. So, let's live out our days in strength and health, and fulfill everything God's calling us to do.

Superintendent Aaron Hlavin: Why wouldn't God heal us of all things? The Bible says to, "Cast your cares on the Lord and he will sustain you" (Psalm 55:22a). However, as we get older, things in our bodies do not work as well. My shoulder does not feel as good as it used to due to an old injury, but I give it to God. I think we can give everything to God, from adoration and success to sickness, pain, and heartache.

Missionary Jared Dietrich: Yes, I believe God can heal anything, but healings for old-age ailments do not happen often.

Pastor Sabrina Chow: I have seen many people healed of arthritis, joint pains, frozen shoulders, even glasses. Once, an elderly lady in my healing class was healed of far- and nearsightedness. She could not read the notes at the start of the class, and after being prayed for, she could read the notes without her glasses.

Pastor Lisa Chin: I think that if God allows it, why not receive it? Be thankful for it, but at the same time learn to grow old graciously. Someday we will all die. As I grow older, I'm believing for healing for my arthritis and I do use reading glasses. I do my best to stay healthy with diet and exercise. If God does heal those things, I will be very happy. But if He does not, I will just live with it.

Apostle Les Bowling: We must accept there is a natural side and a spiritual side. The natural side is you cannot out-train a bad diet. So, you can exercise, but if you are putting all kinds of processed foods

> and toxins inside of you, you are going to ache, you are going to hurt, and it is going to affect your basic health. Also, the outward man is perishing daily, as mentioned in 2 Corinthians 4:16, yet we can be inwardly renewed and healed. I want to live long and strong all my life; however, my outward man is perishing, and I'm losing muscle tissue. So certain things just start to decline in your physical body. That's the natural process. The spiritual side is acknowledging that Moses, at 120 years of age, was still strong and could see well. We also know God heals by His will, so we trust in that, but even the Gifts of Healing will not stop the aging process. I like reading biographies of people who have lived a long life, and they all have "strength." So, that is the thing I pray over people the most: "God, give them strength." Deuteronomy 33:25b tells us that "as your days, so shall your strength be" (NKJV). This means God is the strength for our days, so our days can be increased through our strength.

As we learned from the comments above, God can heal everything, but we must accept the frailty of our bodies, knowing they will continue to degrade until the Lord calls us home to be with Him.

Chapter 15
HOW SHOULD WE NAVIGATE END-OF-LIFE SITUATIONS?

THE PRIORITIES FOR HELPING PEOPLE IN AN END-OF-LIFE OR TERMINAL situation are ensuring peace, comfort, dignity, and respect for their desires throughout their final days.

If the person is an unbeliever, gently, without shame and condemnation, present a simple Gospel message. Realize it may be their last chance to come to know and surrender to Jesus.

Next, if possible, ask the individual exactly what they would like prayer for. Some may want prayer for healing; others may need prayers for relief from pain or nausea; some may want clarity of mind; and others may be ready to go be with Jesus in heaven. Respect their wishes.

What Does the Bible Say About This Question?

Ecclesiastes 3:20: "All go to the same place; all come from dust, and to dust all return."

Psalm 90:10: "Our days may come to seventy years, or eighty, if our strength endures; yet the best of them are but trouble and sorrow, for they quickly pass, and we fly away."

Psalm 90:12: "Teach us to number our days, that we may gain a heart of wisdom."

Psalm 139:16: "Your eyes saw my unformed body; all the days ordained for me were written in your book before one of them came to be."

Exodus 20:12: "Honor your father and your mother, so that you may live long in the land the Lord your God is giving you."

I Timothy 5:8: "Anyone who does not provide for their relatives, and especially for their own household, has denied the faith and is worse than an unbeliever."

I Corinthians 15:42-44a: "So will it be with the resurrection of the dead. The body that is sown is perishable, it is raised imperishable; it is sown in dishonor, it is raised in glory; it is sown in weakness, it is raised in power; it is sown a natural body, it is raised a spiritual body."

Let's Look Deeper:

Most of us have seen others face end-of-life situations, probably starting with grandparents, then parents, relatives, friends, and now maybe even siblings and children. Loss is never easy to bear. When we meet people who are approaching the end of their lives, we should do our best to understand that this is likely the most difficult time in their life, and we should focus on providing peace, comfort, respect, support and dignity.

We know the Bible tells us we came from dust and will someday return to dust (Ecclesiastes 3:20). Moses gave us some parameters in Psalm 90:10, listing a possible lifespan of seventy to eighty years; however, with advances in medicine and clean living, those days are expanded for many. I like how Moses asked the Lord to "teach us to number our days" (Psalm 90:12a). We do not know when our lives will end, but we can live our best lives in glory to God until our end of days. As written in Psalm 139:16, the number of our days is already known by God. I believe that means we should live our best God-honoring lives, and live each day to the fullest. Billy Graham said, "The legacy we leave is not just in our possessions, but in the quality of our lives."[1]

There are a couple more verses I felt were important to include here so we understand what God expects from us in taking care of our aging parents and family members. First, let's look at Exodus 20:12. The verse tells us we will be granted long life if we honor our parents, even if they were not the best parents to us. Most people think this verse applies only to children growing up. However, I believe it is just as important as our parents age, since our roles reverse, and they end up needing care and support from us. It is important to have patience when dealing with aging parents. We shouldn't make any promises we may not be able to keep, such as, "I will never put you in a nursing home." We should also assist them in getting their affairs in order. Encourage them make out their will and trust early, to prevent the senseless fighting later that often goes on between siblings on "who gets what." Also, encourage early drafting of a living will and health care proxy document, so that there is no confusion about their wishes and who will stand up for them should they become so sick they cannot speak for themselves. The entire family should understand any "Do Not Resuscitate/Do Not Intubate" requests in case of emergency. It is difficult to talk about these topics in advance, but the highest form of respect and honor we can give to our loved ones is to allow them to die with dignity according to their own wishes. Often, we need to be their advocates during hospital and in-residence stays to ensure our loved ones are getting the highest quality care. We cannot advocate for our parents or family members well unless we know what they want for themselves, so I believe it is very important to be present in their final years. Paul gave a stern correction for those believers who do not care for their own household and relatives in 1 Timothy 5:8. We have a responsibility to care for our relatives.

We also need to be wise in how long to try to prolong life. Sometimes quality of life is more important than the quantity of days our bodies are "alive." My husband and I just completed our living wills and took a stand on not having extreme life-saving measures. My daughter Leia, who is both an emergency room and ICU doctor, has seen families do everything they can to keep someone alive, and then that person is left with a terrible quality of life afterward. For me, I would rather be with Jesus in heaven than to live a prolonged life in pain, unable to communicate or care for myself, or not knowing who my family is. I recommend spending some time in deep prayer and doing your own research about what you want for yourself when this time comes.

There are many unbelievers who think they will have time for a deathbed conversion and salvation, and it is sad when they die before that happens. My heart grieves whenever I attend a funeral service of an unbeliever. Regardless of if we think someone is a believer or not, if given the opportunity, we should always gracefully walk a person in an end-of-life situation through a confession of faith in Jesus Christ. If they claim they are a nonbeliever, be bold in telling them about the Lord. Most think their sins are too big to be forgiven, so be ready to share God's love and forgiveness. Sharing your own testimony is also a good way to open someone's heart to receive Jesus. See the appendix to guide you as you pray with them.

Can someone on their deathbed be healed? Yes, but that rarely happens. We can have the strongest faith imaginable, but that doesn't mean someone is going to be healed. In 2007, when my mom went through her pancreatic cancer battle, I had just finished a Kenneth E. Hagin course on healing, and I had the faith to believe in healing for her. I prayed over her, laid hands on her, anointed her with oil, and believed in faith for her healing. In my mind, I was convinced God would heal her. However, it didn't happen. While we were in the hospice facility, the nurse said to me, "Her body is shutting down, so you have to let her go, and then you have to tell her it is okay for her to go." That was difficult, as my mom and I were very close, and I wasn't ready to lose her. It took some time in prayer with the Lord, but eventually I told my mom it was okay for her to leave me and go to heaven. I released her to the Lord. She lived only another few hours, then passed away in my arms while I was reading to her from the Bible. Later, I asked the Lord, "Why wasn't my mom healed when I had the faith to believe for her healing?" He told me, "It was her time to go; she lived a good long life." God called her home. Recently, I came across a Facebook post calling for healing prayers for a ninety-year-old retired minister. I prayed for him but also prayed his family would release him to go home to the Lord and leave his pain behind. Paul gave us a wonderful glimpse of what is in store for believers in 1 Corinthians 15:42-44. What a joy to know when we pass, we will receive everlasting spiritual bodies full of glory and power.

When you have the opportunity to pray for someone nearing the end of their life, do your best to bless them. Find out what specific prayers you can pray for them to relieve any suffering. Pray over anything that is making them uncomfortable, and pray they have clarity of mind to remember and recognize family members. Let them set the pace of your visits and what they would like to talk about. This is a great time to let them know how much you love and appreciate them, sharing good stories and telling them how they blessed others along the way.

I believe it's acceptable to pray and ask the Lord to take those who are suffering to heaven; however, I believe life is a gift from the Lord, and it is not within human authority to end a life. This is a subtle and sometimes difficult-to-understand distinction and can differ between denominations. My Assemblies of God denomination opposes physician-assisted suicide or euthanasia for any person, which I agree with. However, we emphasize the value and dignity of every human life, regardless of physical condition. We should acknowledge the suffering of the terminally ill and advocate for palliative care, comfort-only focused care, and compassionate support.

Let's hear some excellent points from a few of our ministry leaders on this topic:

> **Apostle Naomi Dowdy**: There is a great mystery about why some people are healed and others are not. No one is going to escape death; we're all headed there. If you feel led to pray for healing, keep praying, and don't get discouraged or give up hope. Our bodies are in a constant state of decay, from the moment we're created in the womb straight through toward the grave. It's a journey we all take. So, don't be discouraged when you pray and contend for someone, and they pass into glory in heaven. That is a win in some ways. I can tell you hundreds of stories of praying with people fighting against a disease, then seeing miracle breakthroughs, but also eventually burying them. They were blessed that God have them an extension in their lives. That's the great dilemma we live in. We're not in the Garden of Eden anymore, but we're in this broken, messy world. However, we're pressing toward the time of Jesus returning.

> **Superintendent Aaron Hlavin**: There is not enough teaching on end-of-life situations in the church today. Whenever I approach a family in that situation, I first ask the person how they want me to pray. And if the person says, "I want the Lord to take me," I switch my prayers from healing to going to be with Jesus. So, "Lord, bring this to an end." If the person is unable to communicate, I follow the lead of the family, but ask if they are praying in line with what that person wanted. If it's healing, I will continue to pray for that until they are recovered or passed on. I

remind the family that if they don't get healed medically, progressively, or miraculously, then as believers there's a 100 percent chance they will be healed eternally. That way they're not blaming themselves, or God. They're just waiting on God's timing to do it. This provides peace for people going through end-of-life situations. It's not that they lost the fight; it's that they gained eternity in heaven. We made that part of our staff training and counseling sessions. If someone came to us at the beginning of a cancer diagnosis, we would say, "Yes, God's going to heal you. We hope it's medically, progressively, or miraculously. If not, just know God's guarantee to the Christian is healing eternally." I've had people on their deathbeds tell me, "Thank you for saying that at the beginning; it prepared me for all four options."

It's important when helping people facing end-of-life situations not to let them become overwhelmed with guilt and condemnation. Often, they will think this is God's punishment for some sins in their past. Remind them, once we ask the Lord to forgive our sins, they are forgiven, and He remembers them no more (Hebrews 8:12). Sadly, I have seen other believers shame them and ask them about sins from their past. They also can receive attacks from Satan telling them, "Well, you did 'this' wrong ten years ago, or maybe you have this hidden sin in your life that no one knew about, or this is your fault." Sadly, I've watched godly people spend the last months of their life miserable, struggling in their faith, feeling condemnation, and that is painful to watch. It is always best to help people keep their focus on Jesus, and not on their past. Someone once said, "If we focus on what's right in the world, we will have the energy to fix what's wrong, but we are so focused on what's wrong, we don't have the energy to fix anything." I think the biggest tragedy is people struggling under condemnation they created for themselves. Let's help them understand God's love and forgiveness. Let's pray for them to contend for healing and not to give up too soon.

We need to remember how much better it will be for believers in heaven. When my mom, Karen Hlavin, faced her end-of-life situation from cancer, I told her, "I'm going to really miss you, Mom." I was 100 percent a mama's boy and talked with her at least once every day. Her response reminded me about how great eternity would be for her. She said, "Sorry, honey, after I'm gone, I probably won't miss you at all. The minute I die, I'm not going to care about this body. I'm not going to care about the cancer. And honestly, I'll not miss any of you, since I'll be in the presence of Jesus, in the greatest place ever." My mom taught me how to die. I'd never seen anybody in my life just so focused on God and thankful about His goodness. I was glad my mom modeled God's love through her painful final days.

Pastor Walt Landers: Sometimes I feel we have lost the art of dying well. The side effect of believing that healing will come for every single person we pray for is we don't accept the eventuality of death. Everyone will die, and sadly, many before they reach an old age. Even all the famous faith healers in the last one hundred years have died or will die at some point. So, how do we wrestle with the tension of praying for healing, but also allowing people to accept this may be the end of their life? If they desire prayer for healing, then stand with them until their dying breath. Help them to die well and feel the peace of going to be with Jesus, where there is no more pain and sorrow. Let's operate in the fruit of the Holy Spirit–love, joy, peace, gentleness, and kindness– when praying with people in end-of-life situations.

Pastor Jim Westheim: Age has its limits. When I'm at the hospital and a family says, "Please pray for healing for my dying ninety-year-old mother," I will go over to that elderly person, if they are conscious, and ask them how they want me to pray. Nine times out of ten they say, "I want to go home to be with Jesus." Then, we need to help that family see the bigger picture: the greatest healing is up in heaven with Jesus. So, it can be a tough prayer for the family. When a believer is sick, even unto death, that process can be a beautiful thing for others to see and be encouraged by. It can give others hope and may lead others to accept Christ. It's a beautiful thing to sit at the bedside of a believer, whether they are young or old, as they step into the presence of God, knowing the wonderful place He has prepared for them. It is a wonderful thing even though you feel the loss and the family is grieving. We wouldn't want them to come back to this earthly life.

In summary, respect the desires of the person facing their end-of-life situation. Pray as they desire, ahead of family desires. Help people not to face shame or condemnation about their past lives but to know the love and forgiveness of our Lord. If possible, make sure unbelievers have one more opportunity to surrender to Jesus and spend their lives in heaven. Let's help people die well.

Chapter 16

ARE PEOPLE STILL RAISED FROM THE DEAD TODAY?

Yes, people are still raised from the dead. However, it was very rare in the Bible, and it is very rare today.

What Does the Bible Say About This Question?
Luke 7:12-15: "As he [Jesus] approached the town gate, a dead person was being carried out—the only son of his mother, and she was a widow. And a large crowd from the town was with her. When the Lord saw her, his heart went out to her and he said, 'Don't cry.' Then he went up and touched the bier they were carrying him on, and the bearers stood still. He said, 'Young man, I say to you, get up!' The dead man sat up and began to talk, and Jesus gave him back to his mother."

Matthew 9:18-19, 23-25: "A synagogue leader came and knelt before him and said, 'My daughter has just died. But come and put your hand on her, and she will live.' Jesus got up and went with him, and so did his disciples. . . . When Jesus entered the synagogue leader's house and saw the noisy crowd and people playing pipes, he said, 'Go away. The girl is not dead but asleep.' But they laughed at him. After the crowd had been put outside, he went in and took the girl by the hand, and she got up."

John 11:43-44: "When he had said this, Jesus called in a loud voice, 'Lazarus, come out!' The dead man came out, his hands and feet wrapped with strips of linen, and a cloth around his face. Jesus said to them, 'Take off the grave clothes and let him go.'"

Act 9:40-41: "Peter sent them all out of the room; then he got down on his knees and prayed. Turning toward the dead woman, he said, 'Tabitha, get up.' She opened her eyes, and seeing Peter she sat up. He took her by the hand and helped her to her feet. Then he called for the believers, especially the widows, and presented her to them alive."

Acts 20:9-10: "Seated in a window was a young man named Eutychus, who was sinking into a deep sleep as Paul talked on and on. When he was sound asleep, he fell to the ground from the third story and was picked up dead. Paul went down, threw himself on the young man and put his arms around him. 'Don't be alarmed,' he said. 'He's alive!'"

Let's Look Deeper:

It is rare to find biblical examples of anyone raised from the dead, other than Jesus Christ. It was only recorded three times in the Old Testament. First, Elijah the Prophet raised a widow's son from the dead (1 Kings 17:17-24). Then his protégé Elisha the Prophet, who had the same anointing, brought back the son of a Shunammite woman (2 Kings 4:18-37). Then, there was the unusual circumstance where a dead man returned to life when his body touched Elisha's bones after being put in his grave (2 Kings 13:21).

Even in the New Testament, it was a rare occurrence. Jesus healed hundreds, maybe thousands, of people throughout His short three-year ministry, yet He only raised three people from the dead, as seen in Luke 7:12-15; Matthew 9:18-19, 23-25; and John 11:43-44. Both Peter and Paul were in ministry over thirty years, and each of them only raised one person from the dead, as seen in Act 9:40-41, and Acts 20:9-10.

From my research, praying to raise someone from the dead should only happen when you are strongly led by the Holy Spirit. Of the twenty ministry leaders I interviewed, only three were a part of someone being brought back from death. In all cases, it happened just after the individual passed away. For the other seventeen ministry leaders, most said they had never felt the Holy Spirit urge them to pray for that, even when praying for those near death. So, raising people from the dead rarely happens today and, as discussed in the prior chapter, should typically not be our focus when praying with people at the end of their lives. However, we can continue to hope and believe for miracle stories like those listed below.

Director Jill Boyonas: Early in my ministry I was an evangelist and was invited to a remote location in the Philippine mountains. It was a small Chrisitan community, surrounded by Muslims, unbelievers, and many witch doctors. We had a good crowd for our first two days of meetings, but there was no move of God nor any revival among the people. Then I noticed everyone, including the pastor, was wearing the same strange amulet necklace. They said the amulets were given to them by the local witch doctors to protect them from evil spirits. I confronted the pastor and the people, and reminded them the amulet was not from God but was a demonic item. I told them everyone must take off that amulet, or I'd stop the meeting and depart the village. Everyone agreed to remove them, so we had a cutting ceremony and burned everything. After that, the Spirit of God moved mightily among the crowd; many of them got saved, and many of them were filled with the Holy Spirit. Later that evening we held a night service, and the presence of God was so sweet.

As I was worshipping somebody touched my back and said, "Pastor, someone needs prayer in the kitchen," and I responded, "After I finish preaching." They came again, and I delayed them again. The third time they told me, "Someone died in the kitchen." So, I ran to the kitchen, and there was the lady cook, dead on the floor. I checked, but no breathing and no heartbeat. Immediately, the devil started whispering to me, "They will blame you, and they will kill you. You asked them to take off the amulets, and now a lady is dead, so you will be the next to die." I started praying and casting out the spirit of death. Nothing happened. I came to the end of my rope and said, "Lord, if I die, I die." Right after I said that, from deep within my belly, I felt a flow of the Holy Spirit. I started speaking in tongues; immediately those around me were baptized in the Holy Spirit and spoke out loud in tongues. Then, suddenly, the dead lady cook just stood up. So, we asked her, "What happened?" She said, "I know I was dead, because I fell, and I knew I was leaving my body, going up. And I heard everyone saying how much they liked me, and that I will be missed. There was great joy in my heart, because I was on my way to heaven to be with Jesus. But then I saw the faces of my two young kids beside my body crying. I was debating whether to go back or to go up to heaven. I decided to go back for my kids, but I could not-not until everyone started praying in tongues. Then I was back in my body, and I woke up."

So that is my experience, and I do not take credit for that because it was all God.

Apostle Lana Heightley: In the year 2001, my ministry, Women With A Mission, held an outdoor tent meeting for over three hundred women in Sri Lanka. It was very hot, and during a break, my team and I were under some trees having a cool drink. Then, we heard a loud scream, and somebody ran over to us and said, "A woman just died in the tent!" Some other ladies picked her up and carried her to our tree. One of the attendees was a medical doctor, who examined her, and she said, "Ma'am, I'm sorry, she's gone. She died. She's with the Lord." But the Holy Spirit rose up in me, and without thinking I started commanding in a loud voice, "Satan, you take your hands off this woman! In the name of Jesus, I declare life!" Nothing immediately happened, but I felt led by the Holy Spirit to keep going, so I started yelling at the enemy again: "You have no legal rights. She is a child of God. I speak life. I call her back in the name of Jesus," and I just start saying, "Jesus, Jesus, Jesus." Then, the woman suddenly came back to life and started coughing. The doctor took care of her, and she was back in service that night. In these end times that we are living in, we should have the faith to believe God will use us to do these kinds of miracles. God's people are going to have stronger faith. They need to be encouraged and know that God answers even in death.

Mr. Worldwide Evangelist: The first time God used me to bring someone back from death was during my Oral Roberts University years. Another friend and I took a classmate to the emergency room (ER), as he was having severe back pain. As we were with him in the ER, right on the other side of his curtain was an elderly lady hooked up to all sorts of IV lines, with breathing tubes going up into her nose. There was enough of a gap in the curtain where I could look at her. For a while she was moaning and groaning. Then, suddenly, she went silent, exhaled loudly, and we heard the flatline of the heart monitor. They called a Code Blue, and all these doctors scrambled in and started working on her. It was clear they were losing her, and no heartbeat was coming back. I knew it was time to pray. So, I just stretched out my hand, and I commanded life to come back into her, because nothing they were doing was working.

I said a brief prayer of speaking life, rebuking death, right through the curtain, and I said, "In Jesus' name, amen." Right then I heard the beep, beep, beep as the heartbeat started up.

The other time was the along the Amazon in Peru. I was leading a large group of teenagers on a mission trip. After several days on a boat going down the Amazon, the kids were taking a break and horsing around alongside the river. One of the teenagers hit her head, but she didn't tell us. A little later she went out to do drama evangelism with her team, but her team leader had to carry her back because she was stumbling and falling. We raced to the only medical facility nearby, a little jungle outpost clinic. It was very small and very meager in its tools and resources. The doctor checked her out and said she needed to be taken back to a major city where she could get real help, as it was very serious. At first, we thought it was just a concussion, but while she was lying there in that little clinic, we watched as the color in her face completely changed, her eyes rolled back into their sockets, and she passed out. In that moment, she turned this grayish ashen color. You could sense that death was coming. As she exhaled her last breath and her heart stopped, something rose up in me. And I just said, "In the name of Jesus, you're going to live and not die. I rebuke you, death; you leave her." And as quick as all those things happened, she gulped for air, and her eyes flew open. She gulped for air again, her color began to return, and she lived.

So those are the two accounts—both were right at the door of death, and each had only been dead minutes or seconds. But still, the power of God was amazing in those moments. So, praise God!

Superintendent Aaron Hlavin: I haven't witnessed someone being raised from the dead, nor do I know people who have had that experience. But I've noticed a common thread in those who've been a part of it. They take the act of someone being raised from the dead in stride, in the same vein as the person who got healed from a wheelchair, or a person that got a shoulder healed, or a girl with chronic migraines or whatever. They consider it just another miracle from God.

To sum up this question, raising people from the dead was rare in the Bible, and few have been a witness to it or prayed for it to happen today. If you feel strongly led by the Holy Spirit to pray for this, then do not deny any move of the Spirit and pray as the Holy Spirit leads you. Though they are rare, we can still pray and believe for these kinds of miracles from God.

Chapter 17

HOW DOES DEMON DELIVERANCE FACTOR INTO HEALING?

THERE IS STILL DEMONIC ACTIVITY IN THE WORLD TODAY, AND PEOPLE are still being delivered from demonic influences. Some sickness can be from Satan, but not all sicknesses. If someone has a sickness due to a demon, that demon must be put out before praying for healing.

What Does the Bible Say About This Question?

Matthew 8:16-17: "When evening came, many who were demon-possessed were brought to him, and he drove out the spirits with a word and healed all the sick. This was to fulfill what was spoken through the prophet Isaiah: 'He took up our infirmities and bore our diseases.'"

Matthew 12:43-45: "When an impure spirit comes out of a person, it goes through arid places seeking rest and does not find it. Then it says, 'I will return to the house I left.' When it arrives, it finds the house unoccupied, swept clean and put in order. Then it goes and takes with it seven other spirits more wicked than itself, and they go in and live there. And the final condition of that person is worse than the first. That is how it will be with this wicked generation."

1 Corinthians 10:21: "You cannot drink the cup of the Lord and the cup of demons too; you cannot have a part in both the Lord's table and the table of demons."

Galatians 6:1: "Brothers and sisters, if someone is caught in a sin, you who live by the Spirit should restore that person gently. But watch yourselves, or you also may be tempted."

Acts 16:16-18: "Once when we [Paul and Silas] were going to the place of prayer, we were met by a female slave who had a spirit by which she predicted the future. She earned a great deal of money for her owners by fortune-telling. She followed Paul and the rest of us, shouting, 'These men are servants of the Most High God, who are telling you the way to be saved.' She kept this up for many days. Finally Paul became so annoyed that he turned around and said to the spirit, 'In the name of Jesus Christ I command you to come out of her!' At that moment the spirit left her."

Leviticus 19:31: "Do not go to mediums or fortune-tellers for advice, or you will become unclean. I am the Lord your God." (NCV)

Acts 19:13-16: "Some Jews who went around driving out evil spirits tried to invoke the name of the Lord Jesus over those who were demon-possessed. They would say, 'In the name of the Jesus whom Paul preaches, I command you to come out.' Seven sons of Sceva, a Jewish chief priest, were doing this. One day the evil spirit answered them, 'Jesus I know, and Paul I know about, but who are you?' Then the man who had the evil spirit jumped on them and overpowered them all. He gave them such a beating that they ran out of the house naked and bleeding."

Luke 9:1: "When Jesus had called the Twelve together, he gave them power and authority to drive out all demons and to cure diseases."

James 2:19: "You believe that there is one God. Good! Even the demons believe that—and shudder."

Let's Look Deeper:

There are a few things we should address about this subject as it relates to healing, but I will only briefly cover demon deliverance in this book. If you are interested, there are a great many books about demon deliverance.

One of the focuses of Jesus' ministry was freeing people from spiritual bondage, often tying healing with demon deliverance. Per Ed Melick's book *Healing Plunge*, throughout the New Testament, there were seventy-five ailments healed, and fifteen of those were related to demons or evil spirits being cast out.[1] When you study the Gospels, there are many accounts of Jesus and his disciples freeing people from demons and evil spirits (Matthew 8:16-17 is one example). In many cases physical or mental healing occurred when the evil spirit was driven away by Jesus or in the name of Jesus.

Earlier in this book, we discussed how sin can lead to sickness, and sin will open the door for Satan's attacks. Here's a great explanation from David Diga Hernandez:

> So what do we mean when we say, "open door"? Even though the term itself isn't found in Scripture, the biblical principle most certainly is. Simply put, an open door is anything that would give the enemy the upper hand in your life or that would cause you to lower your guard against the lies of Satan. An open door is anything in your life that makes you more susceptible to deception. Another way to word it: an open door is anything you do, say, feel, or think that makes you more receptive to demonic lies. Open doors are spiritual weak points that the enemy can exploit to bring you under the power of deception. Even after you're born again and even if you've already been delivered from a certain bondage, you must maintain a healthy vigilance, for demonic beings are quite persistent.
>
> Beware, demons return to check for weak points. They come back to check on you. When an evil spirit loses a place of influence, it comes back in an attempt to reclaim what it can. In the case of the unbeliever, a demonic being can return to gain full influence, including actual possession. In the case of the born-again believer, who is not "empty" as mentioned in the passage from Matthew 12:43-45, the demon can still return but is limited on what it can do. When a demonic being returns to find influence in the life of the believer, it can come back to attack and deceive–but never again to fully possess, enter, or attach itself to the believer's being in any way whatsoever. The demon has to settle for attacking the believer from the outside.
>
> Still, the demon will take what it can get, so that doesn't mean you can just drop your guard or live in compromise. Demons don't need to

able to fully possess Christians in order to deceive them. For the sake of spiritual vigilance, we ought to consider this important question: why would a demon even need to possess a believer who chooses to live according to its lies? A demon doesn't need to be able to control your body if it can influence your thoughts through deception. So even though the demon cannot literally re-enter the believer's being, it will still return to deceive. For the believer, open doors can never lead to possession, but they can lead to deep deception. That's reason enough to live with spiritual vigilance and to watch for these "open doors."[2]

The Bible says we cannot live a double life, with one foot in the world following Satan and our other foot in church proclaiming to be righteous. Look at what Paul wrote in 1 Corinthians 10:21: "You cannot drink the cup of the Lord and the cup of demons too; you cannot have a part in both the Lord's table and the table of demons." At times, we need to help new believers in this area, as it will take discipleship to help them transition from the ways of the world to the ways of the Lord. Discipleship involves helping believers to grow in knowledge and maturity with the Lord. Also, we should be bold if we see fellow believers going down a dark path (Galatians 6:1). I encourage every believer to have an accountability partner, someone to help you talk through areas of temptation and stay on God's perfect path.

There are other activities that will open the door to demonic influences in our lives. Acts 16:16-18 tells the story of Paul driving out a fortune-telling spirit from a woman. I feel too many believers casually think it's entertaining to visit fortune tellers, attend a palm reading, view tarot cards, and even consult horoscopes. God would never use any of these methods to speak into our lives, so we need to realize they can be traps of Satan, attempting to give us guidance different from God's Word. Leviticus 19:31 makes it clear we should never do that. Doing these things will damage our spirit and possibly our soul. I believe demons can come into unbelievers, but I don't think a true believer can be possessed by a demon. However, both believers and unbelievers can and will be tempted by Satan and his demons. So, be ready, and tell the devil to flee in the name of Jesus when tempted.

Demons can also attach themselves to items and locations. I always anoint hotel rooms, cruise ship rooms, or a new home with anointing oil to cast out any lingering demonic activity. One time, my daughter and I were on a Caribbean cruise, and we visited a local market to get some souvenirs. She woke me up in the middle of the night due to a terrible nightmare; we prayed and went back to sleep. Then I had the exact same nightmare. So, we took out every article of clothing and souvenir we had bought that day and anointed them all with oil and cast out any demons. We didn't have any more nightmares after that.

I have witnessed a few demonic manifestations throughout my years doing ministry, but only in the role of prayer support. The story in Acts 19:13-16 shows this is not something that should be done in a casual manner. If you feel called in this area, I recommend additional education and training in demon deliverance.

All the ministry leaders I interviewed confirmed demonic activity still exists today and can lead to sickness, often the result of sin. Let's review the thoughts of a few ministry leaders on this subject:

> **Apostle Les Bowling**: If a demon is involved with a sickness, it must be removed. A demonic entity can oppress, and a spirit of infirmity can afflict. Healing is never going to manifest until that is dealt with. That entity must be bound and put out of the person, by taking authority in the name of Jesus. A spiritual healing must take place before any soul and physical healing can happen. However, be careful to rely on the Holy Spirit in this area. Once I was doing ministry on a remote island, and a family brought us their son, claiming he was demon-possessed. So, everybody got worked up, and they started praying loudly for this child to cast the demon out. However, one of my team members realized the child was autistic, and that didn't mean he had a demon. Sadly, the child got freaked out by all the yelling and proclaiming, and the parents left in shame and condemnation. It was awful to see nothing good come out of it, especially since neither God's glory nor His love was revealed. Be careful to rely on the Holy Spirit before casting out any demons.

> **Director Jill Boyonas**: The Bible says the enemy wants, "To steal, kill, and destroy" (John 10:10a), so that's his motivation. He would certainly use our physical body to steal health from us. How many people have joy in their life stolen away because they are sick? I think it can be a direct influence of some kind of demonic realm, but it's not always so.

Not every sickness is demonic, but every sickness is a result of the Fall of Man. Sickness is not by God's design, but it's a result of living in a world that's being controlled by darkness. Disease is certainly not a product of Jesus.

Apostle Lana Heightley: I believe in two ways of spiritual deliverance. One is a casting out of demons, and the other is living out the Word by renewing the mind. In the Bible, Paul wrote thirteen epistles which all talked about not giving the devil an open door in our lives. We must keep our minds and spirits renewed with the Word of God (Romans 12:2). Sometimes there are demons that must be cast out. When I was working in the Philippines, we often had to do that. When I did, I always gave that person a paper on how to stay clean, to fill their mind with the Word of God and not allow the demons to return.

Superintendent Aaron Hlavin: I absolutely believe in demonic activity. This is another area we don't do enough teaching on in the church in America. I just don't like to mix healing and demonic activity in the same category. I think there are demonic strongholds on people's lives that cause them harm to their body through sinful actions. We need to remember, the devil is a defeated foe, as Jesus defeated Satan at the cross. The Word says demons flee at the name of Jesus. We know that at the end of time, the devil will be cast into the lake of fire by Jesus. So today I think the devil gets too many talking points in Christians' lives. We have built him up to equal authority with God, and he's not. When I was a lead pastor, new believers would say, "The devil is after me." My reply was, "Of course he is, you're a believer, and you're taking ground for God. He will always be after you, but you shouldn't be afraid." We need to remember the devil is not equal to Jesus and never has been. I'm concerned when every ailment gets tied to a demonic activity, because we're elevating the devil and his authority. And I think we need to recognize he's already defeated. So, keep your eyes on Jesus, not the devil.

Pastor Walt Landers: There is demonic influence that causes us to be sick. We know that the Gerasenes demoniac was out of his mind while under the influence of a legion, or a thousand demons (Mark 5:1-20). I have not encountered that in my ministry, but I have a friend right now who is going through mental health challenges. Her doctors have told her it's a chemical imbalance. So, there are ways doctors can medically treat people for their brains to behave better. So, can there be a direct correlation between the demonic and our bodies being sick? Yes, but it's not always caused by demons. I think there are godly, pure-hearted people walking in freedom who get it, and then there are people who have demonic influence on their lives that get sick. I think both are true.

Pastor Powell Lemons: I believe there are two levels. On one level, I attribute most sickness to natural disorders, caused by germs, accidents, or aging. On the other level, I think demonic power does cause a sickness. Sadly, the Christian community often gets confused on how to pray. Should they pray for healing, or should they pray for deliverance? Too often they're praying for deliverance when they should be praying for simple healing, and vice versa. We need to trust the Holy Spirit to teach us the difference.

Missionary Mary: Some sickness can be brought on by demonic oppression or possession, but not all healing requires a demonic deliverance. Some sicknesses are simply the natural result of our fallen world. However, there are some sicknesses that are very specific to demonic presence. The Gospels list many stories of Jesus casting out the deaf or mute spirit, and then the person was healed. When we pray for someone and sense a demonic presence, we should first take authority over the spiritual dominion. If we only pray for healing, they could be healed but still have the demonic oppression. It is similar to putting a Band-Aid on the problem. The root cause is still there, and the demon needs to come out for complete healing. Spiritual discernment is required in that kind of situation.

Bishop Micheal Pfeifer: Jesus especially wanted to heal people who were touched by the evil one. And that's why there were many incidents where Jesus would release people from the presence of the devil and from his demons. In fact, when Jesus sent out His first disciples, He gave specific instructions: share His Gospel, to bring His healing and mercy to others as they were inspired by the Holy Spirit. Then, Jesus told them to lay hands on the sick and they would be healed, and to drive out demons, healing people from the evil one.

Pastor Jim Westheim: In my mind, demon-possession is not akin to healing. Our bodies are ailing and degrading, and that's what we're asking Christ to heal. Demon-possession is something we are supposed to take authority over. I have seen some outflows of demonic-possession where they have physical manifestations, such as beating themselves against a wall or writhing on the ground. Can God bring healing and deliverance to that? Absolutely.

Mr. Worldwide Evangelist: Jesus took care of both healing the sick and casting out demons. Jesus gave that same authority to His disciples, and to us (Luke 9:1). If a demon is oppressing, possessing, or harassing a person, it must be cast out and commanded to leave. If someone is full-blown manifesting, you must take authority in the name of Jesus, commanding its power be broken over that person. Now the devil plays dirty. Yes, someone can open a door to him. However, sometimes the devil comes in by force, through horrible, traumatic things—whether it's abuse, sexual abuse, molestation, or rape—as just the trauma of those events can open a door for the enemy to come in. If they've done anything to open the door for the demon to enter, they need to verbally repent. They need to ask the Lord to forgive them of any witchcraft-related offense. Then they must shut all doors to the enemy. Above all, remember God loves us. He wants to free humanity if we simply yield to Him, His goodness, His love, and His power.

Pastor Waseem Yousaf: Demons can cause diseases in our bodies. I have seen many times in my ministry where witchcraft and demons destroyed the kidneys and lungs of people so that their bodies would fail to function; and slowly they pass away in a sinful life. Jesus cast out a demon from the woman who was suffering from a humped back (Luke 13:10-17). Jesus cast out a demon from a boy who had a disease like epilepsy (Mark 9:17-29). I think there is no difference in healing the sick and casting out demons from people. One thing is common: we claim the Word of God and apply the blood of Jesus (Mark 16:16).

To conclude chapter 17, there are some different views on the correlation between demonic influence and sickness. Be vigilant in your walk with the Lord and ensure you have not left any open doors for the enemy. Before engaging in demon deliverance, please educate yourself as it is a complex topic and can be a dangerous practice. Above all, make sure you have enough spiritual maturity to understand the situation, as well as enough faith to believe, hear, and trust the Holy Spirit to guide you when you are praying for both healing and demon deliverance. Remember James 2:19 tells us demons believe in God and "shudder," also James 4:7, "Submit yourselves, then, to God. Resist the devil, and he will flee from you." Whenever I feel a demonic presence, I'm quick to bind that demon in the name of Jesus Christ and demand it depart my presence.

Part III:
WHAT ABOUT ME? WHAT SHOULD I DO?

Chapter 18
HOW DO I PREPARE?

H ERE IS A GUIDELINE OF STEPS TO FOLLOW TO HELP YOU PREPARE IN praying for others. More details on each of these steps, with their corresponding scripture verses are provided below:
1. Stay in the Word of God.
2. Be strong and courageous; be ready to share your faith and the Gospel with others.
3. Make prayer, fasting, and communion part of your routine.
4. Ask the Holy Spirit for great faith and the Gifts of Healing.
5. Ask the Holy Spirit for the Gift of Speaking in Tongues to better communicate with him.
6. Review healing passages in the Bible.
7. Read biographies of great Christian healers.
8. Watch and shadow someone who is experienced in praying for healing in others.
9. Start to carry anointing oil with you.
10. Practice on family and friends.
11. Find people to pray for you during the times you will be praying for others.
12. Be humble and do not doubt; only then will the Lord use you to bring healing in others.

Let's Look Deeper:
1. Stay in the Word of God.
John 15:7: "If you remain in me and my words remain in you, ask whatever you wish, and it will be done for you."

This does not need much elaboration. The Word is our source, and we should be reading and studying it every day. This is a requirement for all people involved in any sort of ministry, including praying for others.

> **Apostle Naomi Dowdy:** Really spend time in prayer and the Word to build yourself up in faith, so that you come in faith believing for healing. When you believe in faith, God's promises will come about.

2. Be strong and courageous; be ready to share your faith and the Gospel with others.
Joshua 1:9: "Have I not commanded you? Be strong and courageous. Do not be afraid; do not be discouraged, for the Lord your God will be with you wherever you go."

1 Peter 3:15: "Always be prepared to give an answer to everyone who asks you to give the reason for the hope that you have. But do this with gentleness and respect."

We saw in chapter 5 the importance of faith in healing. The more you trust the Lord to guide you, the more your faith will grow. Do not believe anyone who tells you that you cannot pray for healing in others. The Lord is with you, so you just need to be strong, courageous, and bold in sharing the Gospel, like the Lord told Joshua.

There may be opportunities to share your faith when you pray with someone. In 1 Peter 3:15, Peter reminded us to always be ready, and to share our faith and the message of Jesus Christ with respect. Never miss the chance to share the Gospel or to plant the seed of Jesus' love with everyone for whom you pray. Sometimes, people need to see and hear about God's love up to one hundred times before they finally commit to following Christ. You could be the first or the last; don't give up.

3. Make prayer, fasting, and communion part of your routine.
a. Prayer
1 Timothy 2:1: "I urge, then, first of all, that petitions, prayers, intercession and thanksgiving be made for all people."

Matthew 6:9-13: "This, then, is how you should pray: "Our Father in heaven, hallowed be your name, your kingdom come, your will be done, on earth as it is in heaven. Give us today our daily bread. And forgive us our debts, as we also have forgiven our debtors. And lead us not into temptation, but deliver us from the evil one.""

Prayer is a bedrock for all Christians and should be a part of our daily walk with the Lord. In my daily prayers, I follow the format of the Lord's Prayer (Matthew 6:9-13). I praise God, proclaim His will in my life, ask for my sins to be forgiven, make sure I don't hold any unforgiveness against others, bind the enemy, and then lay out my prayer requests.

b. Fasting
Matthew 6:16-18: "When you fast, do not look somber as the hypocrites do, for they disfigure their faces to show others they are fasting. Truly I tell you, they have received their reward in full. But when you fast, put oil on your head and wash your face, so that it will not be obvious to others that you are fasting, but only to your Father, who is unseen; and your Father, who sees what is done in secret, will reward you."

Matthew 17:21 (NKJV): "However, this kind (of demon) does not go out except by prayer and fasting."

Fasting is another excellent way to connect with the Lord, and it helps us to develop a physical discipline and focus that are useful in deepening our faith. Jesus fasted, Esther fasted, and there are seven other occurrences of fasting in the Bible. In Matthew 6:16-18 Jesus is not saying "*If* you fast," but "*When* you fast," showing us fasting is an important part of our walk with the Lord.

Fasting has significantly deepened my relationship with the Lord over the years. Twice a year, my husband and I go to a prayer and fasting retreat ranch called Praise Mountain in Colorado. I find that during the times in which I withhold food from my body, my spirit and soul are enriched by dedicated time with the Lord. It allows me to hear more clearly from the Holy Spirit, which I put into practice when praying for others. My favorite book on fasting is *Fasting for Spiritual Breakthrough* by Elmer L. Towns.

Fasting can be hard on the body; some medical conditions may make fasting unsafe, or you may require adjustments in your medications. Speak with your physician prior to attempting a fast so it can be done in the safest way possible.

> **Pastor Waseem Yousaf**: When I fast and spend more time praying in the Holy Spirit, there is a correlation to people receiving greater healings. Prayer and fasting build greater faith, which often results in unexpected miracles in the lives of my people.

c. Communion

> **I Corinthians 11:23-25**: "The Lord Jesus, on the night he was betrayed, took bread, and when he had given thanks, he broke it and said, "This is my body, which is for you; do this in remembrance of me." In the same way, after supper he took the cup, saying, "This cup is the new covenant in my blood; do this, whenever you drink it, in remembrance of me.""

When we accept communion, we bring Jesus into our remembrance. Most of us are familiar with taking communion only on Sunday, but there is no biblical reason to limit communion to just once a week. I have taken communion daily when I have been sick, and I took it every day I worked on this book. It's easy to find the communion cups online to have available when you feel led to take communion.

> **Missionary Mary**: Our ministry team takes communion frequently. We acknowledge the power of the blood of Jesus—that He's the one who purchased salvation, healing, deliverance, and restoration—and that everything that we need is really found in the cross. This is one of the powerful ways that we prepare to minister to those who need healing and deliverance. When we pray, we remind ourselves of the victory Jesus won on the cross, and we declare the power of the blood of

> Jesus. When we minister to others we stand in the authority of what He already paid for.

4. Ask the Holy Spirit for great faith and the Gifts of Healing.
I Corinthians 12:31: "Now eagerly desire the greater gifts."

The greater our faith, the greater our capability to heal ourselves and others. We can also ask the Holy Spirit for the Gifts of Healing, with the goal to become a stronger conduit through which the Lord can bring about healing. Review chapters 5 and 6 for more details.

5. Ask the Holy Spirit for the Gift of Speaking in Tongues to better communicate with him.
Ephesians 6:18: "And pray in the Spirit on all occasions with all kinds of prayers and requests. With this in mind, be alert and always keep on praying for all the Lord's people."

I think any true believer can ask for and receive the Gift of Speaking in Tongues. This is a supernatural prayer language you can receive from the Holy Spirit that sounds like you are speaking in a foreign dialect, sometimes with weird sounds. When you pray out loud in tongues, your spirit is speaking directly to God's Holy Spirit. There are many great books available on this if you'd like to know more.

When the situation is amenable, I will pray in tongues in the beginning of my healing prayers for people. I find when I do this, the Holy Spirit imparts to me relevant thoughts and feelings about the person in front of me and why they may have asked for healing. However, you must be sensitive to the environment and whether the person is familiar with speaking in tongues. It can disturb people if they have no idea why you are speaking in that way. It is a tool to help in your prayers, but it's not required when you pray with others.

> **Mr. Worldwide Evangelist**: During ministry I'll always pray in the Holy Spirit. I encourage others that are working with us to pray in the Holy Spirit a little bit too. Prayers in the Holy Spirit get our hearts focused on Him. I will pray in other tongues so that I am supercharged on the inside, building myself up in my most holy faith, so that I am ready for action.

6. **Review healing passages in the Bible.**

2 Timothy 3:16-17: "All Scripture is God-breathed and is useful for teaching, rebuking, correcting and training in righteousness, so that the servant of God may be thoroughly equipped for every good work."

Matthew 10:1, 7-8: "Jesus called his twelve disciples to him and gave them authority to drive out impure spirits and to heal every disease and sickness . . . As you go, proclaim this message: 'The kingdom of heaven has come near.' Heal the sick, raise the dead, cleanse those who have leprosy, drive out demons. Freely you have received; freely give."

Luke 10:9: "Heal the sick who are there and tell them, 'The kingdom of God has come near to you.'"

The more we read about healing in the Bible, the more aware we become of the ways God can bring about healing. The book *Healing Plunge* by Ed Melick tells us there are 343 passages of Scripture on healing for us to study.[1] Most of the ministry leaders interviewed agreed this practice is very important to prepare oneself to pray for others.

> **Pastor Hibroon Khokhar**: We teach our staff and altar ministers all the miracles from the Bible. That encourages and assures them God still does miracles, and it helps them understand the authority Jesus gave them for healing. This way we can build their confidence when they are praying for healing with others.

> **Mr. Worldwide Evangelist**: I believe it is so important to look at the Scriptures when we train believers to walk in anything that God has called us to do. I like to take people to these two important passages: Matthew 10:1, 7-8 and Luke 10:9. With these verses, Jesus was telling His disciples, "You have been around me and watched me; now go forth." It is beautiful because He did not limit His followers to a lesser category of healings and miracles that they could operate in. Jesus did not say, "I am the Son of God and will do the big miracles, and you disciples will do lower-level miracles and only cast out lower-level devils." Instead Jesus said, "You are going to do exactly what I have

done." This was amazing since the disciples at that point were still sinful men. They had not been born again because Jesus had not died on the cross; He had not risen from the grave. So, they could not be new creatures in Christ Jesus until He paid that ultimate price, and then they were re-created. So as believers now, we are in a higher standing than they were with Jesus.

7. Read biographies of great Christian healers.

Learning about great Christian healers of the past, and how they prayed for healing in others, is very educational and motivating. Here is a list of interesting healers to start with: Aimee Semple McPherson, Smith Wigglesworth, Kathryn Kuhlman, John G. Lake, Kenneth E. Hagin, Oral Roberts, F. F. Bosworth, William Branham.

8. Watch and shadow someone who is experienced in praying for healing in others.

I Corinthians 11:1: Paul writes "Follow my example, as I follow the example of Christ."

As with learning any new skill, it is always a good idea to watch others who are experienced to learn from them. Early in my ministry, I never missed an opportunity to watch others pray and minister. I love the familiar quote, "Imitation is the sincerest form of flattery."

> **Director Jill Boyonas**: I think the best way to train believers is to model what to do. We should always bring people along with us. They watch us and work with us, and we guide them on the best ways to pray. We model so they can assist, watch, and learn.

> **Pastor Jim Westheim**: I had a great role model who taught me how to pray for others. Early in my ministry, my model was my home pastor in Minneapolis, Minnesota: Ed Tedeschi. I did hospital visits with him and watched him pray for people for healing. Some were out of the hospital within a couple of days, while others died the next day. Through him, I learned the bigger picture of healing. God's always healing, either here on earth or once they get to heaven. There is a loss, and grief, when

> someone departs this earth, but that's the ultimate healing. So modeling is a big deal, and it's important for believers to be trained in that way for praying for healing.

> **Pastor Lisa Chin**: Whenever I find people who have a heart for the sick, I invite them with me when I go and pray for the sick in hospitals and nursing homes. It is great experience for them.

9. Start to carry anointing oil with you.

Mark 6:13: "They drove out many demons and anointed many sick people with oil and healed them.

James 5:14: "Is anyone among you sick? Let them call the elders of the church to pray over them and anoint them with oil in the name of the Lord."

The Word of God tells us to use anointing oil when praying for people, especially for healing (James 5:14), though there is not a specific biblical reason explaining why to use oil when praying. Most scholars believe the oil represents the Holy Spirit's presence and power. It was used in the Old Testament to designate appointment to the role of king for Saul, David, and Solomon.

It is good to keep your own anointing oil on hand. Most churches will have it available for altar ministry. I always bring it on trips to use when I am praying for people. Remember to always ask the person first if it is okay to anoint them with oil. I use it at the beginning of the prayer, and I will put some oil on my finger and make the sign of the cross on their forehead.

Anointing oil can be found easily online or in Christian stores, but any kind of oil can be used. There are times I have used regular cooking oil, because the power is not in the oil itself but in the strength of your faith. If you are somewhere where anointing oil is not available, just pray and proclaim anyway; the Lord will still heal.

10. Practice on family and friends.

James 1:22: "But be doers of the word, and not hearers only" (NKJV).

Doing anything for the very first time is scary, no matter what it is. However, the more you practice something, the more comfortable you will feel and the better you will be. So, start out praying out loud for yourself. Then pray for your family, friends, even your pets. Many years ago, I started a Bible study in my home. Most of the attendees did not know each other, but I had everyone pray for each other out loud every week. They really didn't like it at first, and most felt uncomfortable and ill-equipped to pray out loud. But as the weeks and years went by, everyone in the group became very proficient and comfortable praying out loud at any time. The more you practice praying for people out loud, the more comfortable you will become.

11. Find people to pray for you during the times you will be praying for others.
   Galatians 6:2: "Carry each other's burdens, and in this way you will fulfill the law of Christ."

Never hesitate to ask others to pray for you, no matter how experienced you become. Galatians 6:2 tells us we need to pray for and support each other. The prayers of others should be considered your greatest strength, not a sign of weakness. For example, I ask my husband to pray for me whenever I preach or teach, and I never leave for an international ministry trip without strong prayer support from my family, friends, mentors, and supporters. I believe there is strong protection and power that come from this support. I have been in many dangerous situations that I believe I navigated through with safety only due to the strength of my prayer support system at home. Be adamant about finding people to pray for you with any ministry you are doing, including altar ministry or praying for family and friends. You will find it is surprisingly easy to find others who will pray for you; just ask.

> **Superintendent Aaron Hlavin:** Early in my ministry I discovered the value of having others pray for me. I was surprised when others approached me and told me they were praying for me. Those prayers sustained me as a lead pastor and now as superintendent of the Michigan Ministry Network.

12. Be humble and do not doubt; only then will the Lord use you to bring healing in others.

a. Stay humble.

Proverbs 11:2: "When pride comes, then comes disgrace, but with humility comes wisdom."

Watch out for pride during any ministry you are doing for the Lord, especially if someone is healed through your prayers. Make sure God alone gets all the glory for the work you do in His name.

> **Missionary Mary:** Since the Gifts of Healing are supernatural, there can be a tendency for ministers to fall into pride. People sometimes start to identify with the gift rather than identifying with Christ. It is very important to remain in relational communion with the Holy Spirit and stay rooted and grounded in God's Word so we will not prey to a spirit of pride.

> **Pastor Waseem Yousaf:** I have seen people try to take all the credit when healing occurs and try to receive honor for themselves, instead of Jesus. That is a huge mistake, and in most cases the healings will stop working when that person is praying.

> **Pastor Hibroon Khokhar:** Healing is only by the name of Jesus. Sometimes believers think the power is in them, and they put themselves first. That is a huge mistake, and then healings will not come.

b. Do not doubt.

Matthew 21:21-22: "Jesus replied, "Truly I tell you, if you have faith and do not doubt, not only can you do what was done to the fig tree, but also you can say to this mountain, 'Go, throw yourself into the sea,' and it will be done. If you believe, you will receive whatever you ask for in prayer."

Jesus told us in Matthew 21:21-22 about the power we have when we believe and do not doubt. God can and will do amazing works through us to bring about healing in others.

> **Superintendent Aaron Hlavin**: When I am preparing to pray, I prepare my emotions by remembering that sometimes it's a twenty-year process of healing. I go in fully expecting God to do what He wants to do, and I'm content with whatever He does. I just go in with optimism, hope, belief, and faith, and I say, "God, it's your people, and you've got a problem in your people. How can I help your people, God?"

> **Pastor Powell Lemons**: Prayer should always be the first choice when someone needs healing—prayer, along with medical options and guidance from our doctors. We are called to believe and agree on God's path for that person. We know not everyone is miraculously healed when we pray for them, so do not put that pressure on yourself when you do not see it immediately happen. We are called to believe, to extend our faith in their direction, and to let God be God in that picture.

In summary, these twelve steps should provide you with a solid foundation as you embark on God's calling to pray for others.

Chapter 19

WHEN AND WHERE SHOULD I PRAY FOR HEALING?

PRAY FOR PEOPLE ANYTIME AND ANYWHERE! PRAY RIGHT WHEN IT'S needed and try not to wait. Always follow the Holy Spirit's prompting to pray for someone who comes to mind.

However, be respectful of the location. If you're at a facility, follow their rules. Also, be sensitive to local customs, especially if you are in a different region or country.

What Does the Bible Say About This Question?

Matthew 18:19-20: "Again, truly I tell you that if two of you on earth agree about anything they ask for, it will be done for them by my Father in heaven. For where two or three gather in my name, there am I with them."

Ecclesiastes 11:4: "Whoever watches the wind will not plant; whoever looks at the clouds will not reap."

Titus 3:1-2: "Remind the people to be subject to rulers and authorities, to be obedient, to be ready to do whatever is good, to slander no one, to be peaceable and considerate, and always to be gentle toward everyone."

Let's Look Deeper:
1. "Now" is the best time to pray.
When anyone you are with asks for or needs prayer, stop everything you are doing and pray with them. Do not wait until later, or for your personal prayer time. Healings are more likely to happen when you are with the person in need, praying beside them. Look at what Jesus said about the power of people praying together in Matthew 18:20: "For where two or three gather in my name, there I am with them." Ecclesiastes 11:4 puts this into perspective. If we wait around for ideal conditions, they may never come. We should be proactive and seize any opportunity to pray with people when they ask or when they need prayer for difficult situations in their lives.

This does not mean that you should never add a person to your prayer list for later, especially if you believe that their healing needs continual support with prayer over a longer period of time. There are times that those in need of your help and prayers are far away from you physically, or you may have no information on what exactly is going on or what needs healing. Over the years my personal practice has evolved to prioritize the requests I am receiving from the Holy Spirit as soon as I hear them. When the Holy Spirit suddenly brings someone to my mind, I stop what I am doing immediately to say a prayer for that person. Sometimes this happens during my quiet prayer time, sometimes while I'm driving in my car. I developed this habit because of the numerous times I was prompted by the Holy Spirit to pray for someone, only to find out later that the person was in a dangerous situation or going through a physical or emotional crisis, and they needed prayer to help them through at that very moment. I've heard similar stories from other fellow believers. I have developed the routine of prayer first, followed by a text to the person to check in. Even if the person reports feeling well, trust that the Lord used you to serve a purpose. Your prayers may have helped them avoid an impending crisis altogether!

It takes spiritual maturity to hear from the Holy Spirit. That comes with dedicated times of prayer, study of the Bible, and the practice of quiet listening to develop a sense for when the Holy Spirit asks you to pray for healing for someone. There are many situations easy to identify in your day-to-day life where your healing skills may be needed. Try to never miss opportunities to bless and pray over people. In my personal life, I always try to end a call or meeting with friends with a prayer over them and what is going on in their lives. Often, the Lord will add to that a prophetic word or vision to edify them and build them up. When I go out shopping, if the cash register lines are long, it gives me the perfect opportunity to ask the people standing next to me in line how they are doing or if they are having a good day. When they say they are having a bad day or their back hurts, I ask if I can say a prayer over them; the answer is usually yes! I always add healing to that prayer. If you are interested in street evangelism, you will find most people passing by are not interested in a lecture about Jesus Christ, but many will allow you to pray over them or their family for any troubles they are going through. Don't miss those opportunities to bless other people.

2. Respect your surroundings.
However enthusiastic you may be, make sure you are respectful of your surroundings. For example, when visiting a hospital or nursing home, let your light of Jesus shine, but follow their rules. You may be there to pray for someone you know, but that does not give you license to visit every room down the hall, unless you are invited by the staff to do so. In medical settings, patient privacy is protected by law, so you should not inquire about specifics of the patient's care or medical conditions. Asking about or even looking at patients you are not registered to visit can result in fines and removal from the premises. If the person who asked for prayer volunteers information about their illness, this is okay, but you must be excessively sensitive to privacy here. Also be sensitive if you're around kids, and don't pray without parental consent. Whether you are at work, school, or a volunteer location, make sure to know and follow their rules. Titus 3:1-2 tells us how to behave.

3. Respect the local customs.
Be respectful and aware of local customs when you are in a new environment, whether it's a new city, state, or country. In international settings, this is exceptionally important, as you may not realize how much you don't know, even if you have traveled to the area before. Speak with a trusted local individual about how your clothing and body language come across, and ask if any adjustments should be made to make those around you more comfortable or to not cause distraction from your purpose there.

For example, when I do ministry in Pakistan, I choose to wear Pakistani clothes and a scarf over my head. I do that as a sign of respect for their culture, as that is the way all women dress, both Christians and those from other religions. I want all the people I work with there to know I respect them and their culture. It's always beneficial to read or ask about local mannerisms and learn what is insulting to another culture. For example, if you cross your legs and show a person from some Middle Eastern countries the bottom of your shoe, it's considered an insult. Also, never assume you can touch another person, even if you are praying with them, especially if they are of a different gender.

Although it can sometimes be difficult to separate ourselves from our country's ideals on freedom of expression in clothing and appearance, showing the locals that you respect them and their culture goes a long way. We must remember the purpose for our travel and how to best achieve our goal of connecting most strongly with those we are there to pray for and see healed.

Let's hear what our ministry leaders say on the importance of praying when and where the Lord desires:

> **Apostle Les Bowling**: Healing only comes when I go for it, when I attempt it, when I speak it, when I build faith up in people. When I don't do that, it doesn't happen, so I make every effort to pray for people whenever and wherever I can.

> **Director Jill Boyonas**: I pray whenever the Holy Spirit leads me. When the Gift of Faith rises up in me, I know it is the Lord leading me to pray, and I become as bold as a lion. That's when I see the greatest number of healings.

> **Missionary Jared Dietrich**: We have seen healings more often outside a church meeting. Especially when we are visiting people or sharing Jesus for the first time.

> **Superintendent Aaron Hlavin**: I've seen healings come about in many different places. Once I prayed for somebody at a gas station, and a short time later they sent me a message that said God healed him. Another time I was in Africa, and while I was praying for someone, a

cow wandered over and started going to the bathroom right at the altar right next to me. As we prayed, God healed him.

Missionary Mary: From my own experience, I have found the more I pray for people, the more healing I see. Much like the principle of sowing and reaping. When we sow much, we reap much. The more we pray for the needs of people and stand on the Word of God and his testimonies, the more faith rises up for healing in the future. Faith comes by hearing the word of God and when we have a backlog of God's faithfulness and testimonies of healing, we can have an expectation that says, "Amen!" "Do it again!

Pastor David Paul: Wherever there is need and desire, we see healings. It could be in the church or a home setting; when there is desire for healing and the faith to believe, healing happens most often—especially when everybody is united in the Spirit of God and believes.

Mr. Worldwide Evangelist: We see healings happen all the time, all around the world, in our large crusade festivals, and in schools and markets in the streets. It's not just me and my wife, but also the many, many people who join our mission trips all around the world. It's because we are strong advocates of God's Word, to obey the Great Commission. Jesus said these signs would follow those that believe. So, we see many miracles happen in our outreaches, our evangelism projects, and in church services. Jesus works mighty miracles, just like He did in Bible days, because He's in us.

Allow God to use you to demonstrate His power and bring healing to anyone at any time in any place. However, take the utmost care to be respectful and follow the rules and customs of the places in which you pray.

Chapter 20
IS THERE A CHECKLIST OF WHAT I SHOULD SAY AND DO?

Here is a general checklist for you to follow when praying for others. Don't worry if you miss a step. The more you pray with people, the more comfortable you will become.

1. Always pray and prepare your spirit and soul in advance.

2. Assess the situation:
    a. If you are in a public setting, speak low and be brief.
    b. If you are at a church, find a quiet location where you will not be overheard.
    c. Analyze if it is a proper setting to pray out loud in tongues.
    d. Be ready to present the Gospel if you feel led in your spirit.

3. Before you start praying:
    a. Consider using breath mints in advance.
    b. Have anointing oil ready—if available.
    c. Greet them with a smile, be friendly and compassionate, and show interest in what they are saying.
    d. Ask for their name—so you can repeat it during your prayer.
    e. Ask if you can pray "with" them—not just "for" them; they have an active part in the prayer.
    f. Explain the healing may come miraculously, medically, progressively, or eternally.

g. Ask them if they are ready to receive from the Lord—so they can be expecting.
   h. Ask what they would like prayer for—if they are unwilling to share details, that's okay, just call it an "unspoken prayer," since the Lord already knows what their problems are, and you are agreeing with them that the Lord will answer their prayer.
   i. Ask them to put their hand on the general area of their body needing prayer.
   j. Ask them if you can put your hand on their shoulder or hold their hand.
   k. Ask them if it is okay to anoint them with oil—if you have some.

4. While praying:
   a. Start out by anointing them with oil—if you have it—making a cross on their forehead.
   b. Lift up the individual's request using their name.
   c. Pray to God in the name of Jesus.
   d. Pray a little in tongues, if you believe the individual is aware of tongues.
   e. Listen for any words or thoughts from the Holy Spirit throughout your prayer.
   f. Thank God for who He is and all He has done.
   g. Pray for God's will in this situation.
   h. Speak simply and plainly—not using overly religious words and sayings.
   i. Bind the enemy over any sickness, telling Satan he is not allowed.
   j. Ask the person to repeat out loud, "I ask for forgiveness for any sins I committed that may have led to this sickness or injury."
   k. Command the individual to be healed in the name of Jesus.
   l. After you pray, ask if they feel any immediate relief. If it is a body part that can move, ask them to move the limb or area to check if they received any relief.
   m. Pray again if needed.
   n. If there is no immediate miraculous healing present, agree with the individual the healing will come medically, progressively, or eternally.

o. If you sense the individual needs emotional healing, see Note 1 below.
p. End the prayer by thanking God for His healing.

5. After the prayer:
   a. Have them repeat out loud, "I am healed"—believing healing will come in the Lord's timing.
   b. Encourage them to see a doctor or counselor if needed.
   c. Remind them to only speak positive words and confessions about their healing.
   d. If possible, give them a list of healing verses to post around their house and proclaim God's healing (see Note 2 below).
   e. Ask them if they have any questions.

Note 1: There are additional considerations when praying for those needing emotional healing. Licensed Professional Counselor Brenda Rogers gives us good things to say when we are helping people process their emotional pain in order to gain emotional healing:

When you pray with someone, express empathy. Say phrases like "I am sorry; it sounds so difficult; I cannot imagine." It also really helps the individual when you show acceptance and normalization, giving permission to the person to be in their current state: "It is okay to be where you are."

When you are praying with someone, you should pray for emotional healing for the WHOLE person, so pray for:
1. **Safe places** to name and experience the fullness of your painful emotions.
2. **Quiet presence** of special people to sit with you in the pain and suffering.
3. **Openness to receive** companionship and service from others.
4. **Deep love and comfort** from the companionship and service given by others.
5. **Self-care and compassion** through sleep, hydration, nutrition, and movement.

We can provide a silent presence, offering to sit and be with that person in their pain and suffering. We can provide companionship, being with that person in their daily life and sending the message: "You are not alone; I'm with you." There are acts of service we can do to bless them, asking about their needs, and extending basic care (dropping off meals, doing laundry, etc.).

Note 2: Here is a list of healing verses I give people after praying for them:
- Exodus 23:25-26
- Psalm 30:2; 41:4; 103:2-3
- Isaiah 41:10; 53:4-5
- Jeremiah 17:14
- Matthew 8:5-8; 8:16-17
- Mark 5:34; 16:17-18
- John 14:13-14
- Acts 3:16
- James 5:14-16
- 1 Peter 2:24
- 3 John 1:2
- Revelation 21:3-4

Chapter 21
IS THERE A CHECKLIST OF WHAT I SHOULD NOT SAY AND DO?

This is a long list of things we all should be careful not to do or say when praying for others.

1. Do not pray for others if your spirit and soul are not right with God. Confess your sins and get right with God before praying with others.

2. Assess the situation:
    a. Believe for healing, but do not expect everyone to be immediately and miraculously healed. (It may come progressively, medically or eternally for believers.)
    b. Do not speak in tongues if the person will not understand what it is.
    c. Do not wear inappropriate clothing (i.e., low-cut tops or showing cleavage for women, tee-shirts with inappropriate language or symbols for both men and women).
    d. Do not have bad breath or be chomping loudly with gum.

3. Before you start praying:
    a. Do not force them to tell you details about their medical condition. General descriptions and unspoken prayers are okay.
    b. Do not touch them without first asking.
    c. Do not promise immediate healing (it may come progressively, medically or eternally).

4. While praying:
    a. Do not speak loud enough that others nearby can overhear your prayer.
    b. No screaming or shouting out loud (see Note 1 below).
    c. Do not shake them.
    d. Do not be too aggressive.
    e. Do not speak negative words.
    f. No platitudes: no "time heals, just forgive"/no cheering up/no taking sides.
    g. No judgment: they are free to have their own perspective and response/"No judgment about this."
    h. Do not ask them what sin they did to get this sickness.
    i. Your prayer is not a counseling session; refer them to a counselor if needed.
    j. Do not believe every illness is demon based and needs deliverance.

5. After the prayer:
    a. Never tell someone they do not need to see a doctor or counselor.
    b. Do not make the person feel it is their fault if healing was not immediate.
    c. Do not shame the person for not being Christian enough to receive healing.
    d. Do not make excuses if the person is not healed right away.
    e. No negative confessions: tell them not to say things like "I'll never be healed."

Note 1: Screaming or aggressive behavior toward the person you are praying for can bring up previous trauma. It could bring up issues from previous authority figures in their past who screamed at them or were aggressive with them.

Part IV:

IS THERE GOOD ADVICE AS I BEGIN THIS JOURNEY OF PRAYING FOR OTHERS?

Chapter 22

WHAT MISTAKES DO BELIEVERS MAKE WHEN PRAYING FOR HEALING?

WOULDN'T IT BE WONDERFUL IF WE WERE ALL PERFECT! Unfortunately, we are not; we have made mistakes in our past and will make more in the future. This chapter highlights many mistakes you can learn from, as seen by our ministry leaders. Most of these points have not been covered in detail in previous chapters.

What Does the Bible Say About This Question:

Psalm 37:23-24: "The Lord makes firm the steps of the one who delights in him; though he may stumble, he will not fall, for the Lord upholds him with his hand."

Ephesians 4:29: "Do not let any unwholesome talk come out of your mouths, but only what is helpful for building others up according to their needs, that it may benefit those who listen."

Let's Look Deeper:

Since we are not perfect, we will continue to make mistakes in our walk with the Lord. The purpose of this book is to encourage all believers to believe in healings and have the faith and empowerment to pray for others for healing. In Psalm 37:23-24, we see the Lord will hold us up when we make mistakes. This section lists some of the mistakes our group of ministry leaders has seen in their ministry, things we haven't covered yet in detail.

Mistake #1: Not Letting God Be God

> **Pastor Jim Westheim**: I think the biggest mistake is when believers don't let God be God. Believers are trying to get people healed instantly and not trusting the perspective and process of God in that picture. Sadly, I have seen believers put people through all sorts of lengthy contortions, and prayers, trying to increase their faith. They promise healing, or they will lay their hand on them and say, "I see your healing," trying to make it mystical for people. But then the person just stands there and nothing happens, no immediate healing. We can believe and hope for instant healing, but that's not always God's way. We are called to pray specifically in faith in Jesus' name and let God do His work. It was beautiful how Christ brought healing to people. He did not always heal their physical need first; He healed what was most important. He would say, "Here is your healing, now go and sin no more." It's that picture of what the priorities are from God's side. We need to let God work through whatever is needed in that person's life. God wants to fix the "who" before He can do the "what." Maybe God is talking to them about certain things in their life that need to be realigned. God may be trying to draw that person into a deeper relationship with Him, through the healing process. When that person matures in their faith, then the answer to their healing becomes evident. So, we do not want to rush God. He has a process; He has a plan and a purpose, and we want the people we are praying for to discover that. It may be instantaneous, so believe for it, but it may be a process.

Mistake #2: Shaming People When They Get Sick

It is okay to believe for 100 percent full healing in the people we pray for. However, it is a mistake when some believers shame people for not getting healed. It is not appropriate to criticize others or ask them what sin they are committing to prevent their own healing. This behavior is not only disruptive to any ministry setting but can result in harm or trauma to the individual seeking healing. That person may end up feeling they are not "good enough" to be healed by God and then never come to the Lord for salvation. We should never tolerate the judging or shaming of others.

> **Superintendent Aaron Hlavin**: I have a heartbreaking story about a young lady from my church when I was lead pastor. She had a few

wild teenage years but then gave her life to Jesus and lived a faithful life for over ten years. She was diagnosed with cancer when she was still young. Unfortunately, someone in her life suggested that she must repent from her past sins because that was what caused her to have cancer. This young woman came to me panicked and said, "What did I do wrong in my life that God is punishing me? I asked for forgiveness years ago and have lived a pure life for the Lord." I told her that God was not punishing her. It was probably because we live in a fallen world, and there were a number of reasons the cancer developed.

Mistake #3: Believing There Is a Set Formula for Healing

Pastor Powell Lemon: I have a pet peeve when certain believers dictate a set formula for healing. They will say, "If you follow these exact steps that previous great healers did, like Oral Roberts, then you can see the same healing results." Or they will write a book, or blog article, that lists the "steps" or "formula to use" to see healing results. Some believers who have a strong Holy Spirit Gifts of Healings may broadcast to believers to "do it my way," then promise they will have the same success in healing. Yes, certain people like Oral Roberts had the Spiritual Gifts of Healing and were able to facilitate many miracles of healing when he laid hands on people. However, not everyone has the Gifts of Healing by the Holy Spirit. It is a mistake to teach people that they, too, can receive that gift by doing steps 1-2-3-4. God is not a machine, in that doing steps 1-2-3-4 will result in automatic healing. It is a mistake to teach everybody that when they pray a certain way, people are automatically healed. It simply does not work like that, as God has His process and His ways.

Pastor Walt Landers: The Word shows Jesus did not heal everybody the same. Today every person is an individual and everybody is different, and their healing may be different. If we are not careful, we may take a silver bullet approach and try to use the same ways and words for everyone. It's not "this one magic thing" that will work every time. So, instead of always using the same approach, we need to really hear the voice of the Lord. Before praying for anyone, we should get before God, check our hearts, and listen to the Lord's guidance.

Mistake #4: Speaking Negative Words over Someone's Health or Their Sickness

We need to remain sensitive about how our words might be perceived to someone who is sick and avoid joking about another person's illness. When I initially heard my pancreatic cancer diagnosis, I told several people as I was trying to process the information and probe others for similar experiences. Here are some comments from others I remember hearing that made me feel terrible and have stuck with me even years later: "Wow, that's terrible; no one survives pancreatic cancer." "It's sad you will die soon." "Is your daughter ready for you to die?" "Who gets all your stuff?" and even "Can I have your bike?" None of those comments benefitted me, nor made me feel better about the struggle I was currently facing.

I am a strong believer in the power of both positive and negative words. Positive words are in line with the fruit of the Spirit, which are "love, joy, peace, forbearance, kindness, goodness, faithfulness, gentleness and self-control" (Galatians 5:22-23a). Negative words bring the opposite. I believe any negative word over your life or situation opens the door for Satan to bring that to pass. Look at Ephesians 4:29: "Do not let any unwholesome talk come out of your mouths, but only what is helpful for building others up according to their needs, that it may benefit those who listen." Even today, I am careful *never* to speak negative words over any situation, or any person, and I caution people around me as well. When someone speaks negative words to me, I am quick to say, "I don't receive those negative words." When we stand strong against negative words over ourselves, our spouse, our kids, and any facet of our lives, we prevent the enemy from coming in. Make sure the words you speak over yourself and others are always positive.

> **Mr. Worldwide Evangelist**: We should never condemn or speak negatively to the person we are praying for. We should always encourage them and speak positive words of life over them as we are praying.

Mistake #5: Limiting God's Work to a Specific Person or Location

> **Pastor David Paul**: A big mistake is when believers only have faith for healing in a certain location, like just in the church building, or think only a specific person can do the healing. It is sad when believers try to box

in God's power to certain locations or individuals. It is sad because we see that happen quite often in Sri Lanka. However, God is so much bigger than a person or a place; He's bigger than any of us can possibly imagine.

Mistake #6: Giving Excuses When Healing Does Not Come
Missionary Jared Dietrich: The biggest mistake I see occurs during a situation when the healing does not immediately happen. Sometimes the person who is praying tries to come up with reasons or excuses for it. Sometimes (while usually not intentionally) the one being prayed for feels they are letting everyone down if they do not give some kind of positive report about being healed. They can feel pressured to tell everyone they were healed when they were not. We need to verify healings and celebrate when they happen. When they don't happen, we need to make sure the sick person feels no guilt or shame about it. Never let blame fall on the person needing healing, for not being healed. Walk with them through the healing process.

Mistake #7: Not Celebrating Healing When It Happens
Superintendent Aaron Hlavin: I've noticed, when doing ministry in countries outside of the United States, people celebrate it when they get healed. After praying for someone who gets healed, they will tell you right away, "Look, I'm healed; I'm good." My experiences in America are quite different. When someone gets healed, they tend to say, "I'm not going to tell anybody for six months, and I'm going to wait and see if this healing really happened." I think that is part of the reason we do not have a sense of the healings God is doing in the United States. Healing is happening, but we just do not know how to talk about it, and we do not know how to celebrate it.

Mistake #8: Not Trusting God to Provide When Healed from a Disability or Income-Generating Illness
Although an illness can cause someone significant distress on a day-to-day basis, sometimes we may encounter people who are hesitant to receive healing because their only income comes from disability payments from the government. This is a very tough situation, and it is not for us to judge other people's decisions when they are struggling for survival in the face of

poverty. When faced with this hesitance to receive healing, I try to remind these people that if God is big enough to heal you, He is big enough to provide for you as well.

> **Mr. Worldwide Evangelist**: I tell people that God always has a way to provide for you. If He is good enough to pay the price for healing and disease to be completely eradicated from your life, He surely has a way to provide for you as well. I call that an identification transformation. You begin to focus on His love and His will for you. Then, focus in on one of the Old Testament names of God, like Jehovah Rapha, God our healer. Then remember that Jesus purchased salvation for all of us by shedding His blood for us. That's how you cause an identity transformation. Now you can start seeing yourself healed, seeing yourself no longer in that wheelchair, no longer picking up that disability check, no longer unable to focus in the classroom because of ADHD, or whatever else you might be facing. You see yourself operating fully whole, having clarity of thought and mind, decision-making abilities, and the ability to act smoothly and easily. Because you focused on Him, and thanked God for it, it will fully manifest.

Mistake #9: Thinking We Need to Perform a Long Healing Prayer Versus a Command Like Jesus Did

> **Missionary Mary**: Believers often get tripped up into thinking they have to do a long or fancy prayer for people to be healed. In reality, when you study the Bible, *Jesus didn't actually pray for the sick. He commanded sickness and demon spirits to go.*

> **Mr. Worldwide Evangelist**: We should not just be praying for people to be healed; it is much more. It's commanding in faith to be healed in Jesus' name right now. It's telling the diseases to go, telling the blindness and deafness to leave, declaring sight and hearing to come, declaring legs to move and walk and lameness to leave. It is not praying and trying to ask God to do something; He already said He would do it. It's declaring as the agent of God—whether a son or a daughter of God, operating on His behalf—that His will for healing will be done. So, it is having that attitude that I am not praying and asking God to do this, but I'm proclaiming His Word for healing.

In summary, don't be ashamed of your mistakes; identify them, learn from them, and move on. Look at what Paul wrote in Philippians 3:13b-14: "But one thing I do: Forgetting what is behind and straining toward what is ahead, I press on toward the goal to win the prize for which God has called me heavenward in Christ Jesus." Feel empowered to share your own mistakes with others to help them learn, and do your best to learn from these common mistakes of others as seen by ministry leaders.

Chapter 23
WHAT IS THE BEST ADVICE AND ENCOURAGEMENT FROM EACH MINISTRY LEADER?

Pastor John AD: Remember that Jesus is the best healer. He is the biggest "medicine" in the world. Most people go to doctors and may get medicine to take every day, but they still do not get "whole" healing, because it is not just physical healing they need. My God wants to heal the whole person, not just the physical disease, because He sees the root of the problem. Some diseases do not belong to the flesh or body but belong to the soul. So, God can heal the soul and the spirit, which no medical doctor can do. God starts healing the spirit, which heals the soul, and through the soul, He heals the body. That is why God is the best doctor and the best healer in the world.

Apostle Les Bowling: First, we need to look at the Scriptures that speak to healing. Read materials and books on healing and listen to testimonies of God healing people. So, in other words, feed your faith for healing, and then do what the Bible says to do. Don't be afraid to lay hands on people for healing. Just believe and trust God. The duty to pray is ours, but the results are God's. So, your duty is to speak God's Word, obey it, lay hands on people, and trust God to do the healing.

Director Jill Boyonas: "Just pray and believe" was something I learned from my mentor, Bishop Bing Gadian. When he was a new believer, he would pray for everyone who was sick and kept doing so repeatedly until finally someone got healed. It was amazing—many people were healed whenever he prayed. Then, he wanted to also be the vessel to raise people from the dead. A short time later, his friend's goat died, and he asked God to use him to raise up the goat. He prayed for the dead goat, but nothing immediately happened, so he left. But five minutes later, somebody caught him and told him that the goat he prayed for was alive. So God used him for that as well.

My advice is to just believe, pray, and know healing will come in God's timing.

Pastor Lisa Chin: The Bible says in James 5:14, "Is anyone among you sick? Let them call the elders of the church to pray over them and anoint them with oil in the name of the Lord." Then in Mark 16:18b, "They will lay hands on the sick, and they will recover" (NKJV). We are to do what the Word says—to lay hands, anoint the sick person with oil in the name of the Lord, and pray for healing. When we pray as a team, there is power in united prayer. When we pray for anyone who is sick, we need to pray in faith believing in God's miraculous and healing power to see the person fully restored to health and wellness. Sometimes there may not be immediate healing, but we trust God for His will.

We can also offer support, along with prayers for the sick person and their family, by providing meals, helping with errands and even finances.

It is our responsibility to pray in faith with expectancy and trust God for healing and His best plan for the individual.

Pastor Sabrina Chow: You just need to simply step out in faith and pray your best prayer. It is the Lord who heals, and our role is to be that willing vessel to be used by Him.

Missionary Jared Dietrich: Simply, you need to just keep believing and praying for healing. I believe that we can grow in healing in time and in our spiritual walk. Healing has a zero percent success rate if we don't step out in faith.

Apostle Naomi Dowdy: Remember, God has already provided for healing. It's in the sacraments of communion, as well as His promises to heal all our diseases. This is part of Christ's atonement, and the Word says, "By his wounds you have been healed," (I Peter 2:24). After you take the bread in communion, you appropriate your healing. So really spend time in prayer, build yourself up in the Word, and build yourself up in faith so that you come in faith believing for healing. Don't be afraid when you pray for people. You can pray for the sick, but God will do the healing. It's God doing His work through you. You must speak the Word in faith, and then the Word releases God's power.

Understand that God operates in His own timing. Jesus healed in God's timing—sometimes right away, sometimes later, sometimes He had to say a prayer more than once. I have friends who take communion over an extended period, and through that they are drawn closer to God and have been healed over time. Above all, our God is a sovereign God. He does what He wants in his time. And we don't always have the answers.

Remember, God didn't tell us to heal people but just pray the prayer of faith for healing. When you pray with others for healing, have them confess their sins and pray against any unforgiveness, as both can hinder healing. Once you complete your prayer, tell the person to stand firm in their belief that they are healed. Tell them not to let others talk them out of receiving their healing. They must hold on to God's promises. If faith comes by hearing, it means they must be speaking, declaring, and believing.

Evangelist Tanveer Gill: First, we need to ask God to give us His power and authority. In Matthew 10:1, Jesus gave His disciples authority "to drive out impure spirits and to heal every disease and sickness." As believers, we have that same authority and only need to ask the Lord for it to operate in our lives.

Second, believers need to have courage. Courage to share their faith, and faith to step out and believe in healing. Courage to pray whenever the Holy Spirit leads them to pray for others. Courage like in Deuteronomy 31:6: "Be strong and courageous. Do not be afraid or terrified because of them, for the LORD your God goes with you; he will never leave you nor forsake you."

Third, we need to encourage our fellow believers. In our fellowship, we like to do healing prayers when we are all together in one group. Our Lord Jesus Christ said, "For where two or three gather in my name, there am I with them" (Matthew 18:20). So, whenever we are together, we are praying in one group, and then Jesus is with us. This encourages all the church, both believers and unbelievers, as they hear and see the works of the Lord within our church body.

Apostle Lana Heightley: My best advice is to remember that Jesus told us how to pray. He told us to declare or to demand it. Just look what Jesus said in John 15:7, "If you remain in me and my words remain in you, ask whatever you wish, and it will be done for you." The word *ask* here actually means "demand," or "to put a demand on it." So, when we are walking with the Lord, then we can ask according to His Word, and Jesus will do it. And that asking is "demanding." It's a prayer of authority. If we ask him according to His will, he hears us, and we know He hears us. So, pray for healing with the authority the Lord has given you as a believer.

Superintendent Aaron Hlavin: First, don't put expectations on people. Don't put pressure on people to declare healings they're not healed from yet. Don't make people feel they're spiritually less because they didn't get immediately healed, or they're still struggling. I tell people, "When you pray for people, pray in Jesus' name, not in your name." You don't command God to do things. Ask God. I say, "Lord, bring healing according to Your will, and do Your thing."

Second, when people are not immediately healed, be comforting. Remind them that healing can come in one of four ways: miraculously, medically, progressively, or eternally when they get to heaven with Jesus.

Third, don't be challenging. You need to approach praying for healing in a manner that builds the believer's faith in God. Pray in a way that keeps their faith strong and establishes a rooted connectedness to the possibilities of God. Don't allow judgment, anxiety, worry, or negative feelings.

Fourth, let people pray over "their" needs and desires, not yours. Have a culture of honesty. Ask them how and what they want prayer for. That's really important for end-of-life prayers. Follow the lead, first of the person you're praying for, and then the desires of the family. Ask them, "What are you praying for?" Pray for that. But don't make them feel responsible to you, as they are not.

Pastor Hibroon Khokhar: Encourage believers to pray for healing by reminding them of God's desire to heal and His power to answer prayers. Pray with compassion, love, and confidence, trusting that God will work in His timing. Be persistent, grateful, and open to the Holy Spirit's guidance as you pray, knowing that healing comes in many forms and God is always listening.

Pastor Didier Kokora: First, understand the church's mission in these end times. Ultimately, in this final season before the return of Jesus Christ, it is the church's responsibility to spread the Gospel to all nations. This missionary zeal should be carried by church leaders and members who feel a sense of urgency due to the second coming of Christ. Additionally, they should engage the new generation in this mission, prioritizing the preparation of children and young people to ensure that the message reaches all age groups.

Next is reviving the desire for healing prayer. How can we awaken a desire among God's people to practice healing prayer for the sick? It is essential to intentionally:

- Restore the foundations of authentic Christian life by preaching repentance and the forgiveness of sins, so that believers can receive the gifts of the Holy Spirit.
- Encourage God's people to return to Him by studying and practicing His Word, ensuring they align themselves with His divine plan for humanity.
- Remind everyone of their status as disciples of Christ, meaning they must imitate Jesus in all aspects–including their responsibility to the sick.
- Raise up a church that prays and fasts regularly, equipping believers to stand against the forces of darkness that seek to keep people under various forms of oppression.
- Promote the sacrifice of Jesus Christ as the only divine remedy for healing, even in the midst of all the advances of medical science. Man treats, but it is God who truly heals the sick.

Pastor Walt Landers: The main thing is to make sure you're familiar with healing. You must also have a strong belief that God's Word is true regarding healing.

We all have different strengths and journeys in life. We are in different stages of our maturity with the Lord. Realize that some people are very strong financially and can trust God and believe for finances, and yet they may struggle in another area. We all are in different stages of our faith to see God use us to heal others. But I believe that every single believer has the capacity and the faith needed to put the Word of God on the inside of them, and then to allow that Scripture to come out in those healing prayers for others. So, whether you're speaking the Word, laying hands on the person, or anointing them with oil, just trust God to use you. Pray and do it in such a way that you allow God to really use you. Romans 10:17 says, "So then faith comes by hearing, and hearing by the word of God" (NKJV). So, pray and have the faith to believe. When you give people the Word, then believe the Word works. When you proclaim God's Word, it takes the pressure off you. Sometimes believers feel unworthy or think, *Who am I to do this?* So, we give others the Word of God and know only God can really save their soul. Whenever I present the Gospel for salvation, I'm expecting the Word is doing the work. So, you need to think in the same way for healing. Stick with the Word of God and don't get off in your opinions.

We also need to be more conscious about this season when people are struggling much more mentally and emotionally-more than ever before. I think that there is a healing that God is wanting to release into the souls of humans, to bring some real healing in those areas.

Pastor Powell Lemons: Constantly read the Scriptures that teach healing.

Reverend Merrily Madero: It's your responsibility as a believer to pray, so just do it-right there and then. If you're talking to a friend or family member, and they mention an area they need healing in their life, stop right then and say, "Can I pray for you right now?" And then pray. If you know someone who's stressed, overwhelmed, or depressed, just ask if you can pray for them. If you're talking to a salesclerk in the store or someone you don't know well, and they mention an ache or pain, ask them if you can pray for them. I've said a lot of prayers with people I don't know in the line at Target, which has blessed them and I've seen it in their faces. So, just say a short prayer. Allow the Holy Spirit to bring

His words to your words. I've had people stop me from telling them about Jesus, but I've never had someone turn down a prayer. A prayer can and will plant a seed of God's truth in their heart and spirit and give them hope about their future.

Next, don't ever take the credit when someone you pray for gets healed. God is the One Who does the healing, so make sure He alone gets the credit. Often, when I'm in a church setting or on the mission field, I'll have the person I'm praying for put their own hand on the area of their body that needs healing. Then, if they say it's okay, I'll put my hand on them. I want them to understand that I'm not doing the healing; the Lord is. I want them to understand that they can put their own hands on themselves and pray for healing. They can then use their hands to pray for others. We should be thankful that the Lord used us as His vessel to pray for healing for someone. But don't allow people to thank you for healing them; give all that glory to the Lord.

Missionary Mary: I always like to remind believers that God only asks us to do what we can do, which is pray for the sick, share the Gospel, show love to others. Then we need to trust Him to do the part we can't do: heal the sick, bring salvation, change lives.

Pastor David Paul: I think the best advice is just to believe in the One Who heals. We all need to speak words of faith about our healing. When we have healing services at our church, I always start and end with an encouragement. I always tell them, "Don't go back home and just say that Pastor David prayed for us. Go and tell others that God healed us. Talk about the God Who healed you and believe in the One who heals."

So, when you pray for others, believe they will be healed. The more you pray, the more your faith will grow to believe in healing for others. Don't go out there and just try once for someone who is very sick and dying. Start out praying for your own headache. When a headache comes, lay hands on yourself to pray for yourself. I always tell even the kids here, "First try praying for your pet." Pray for your cat or pray for your dog. Then, pray for someone in your home. I can guarantee you the Lord will heal. When you see a miracle happening in your own home, it will give you faith and strength to go out there and pray for others.

Next, pray for your neighbor or someone in the street. You will see your own faith grow. Keep knocking and praying, trusting in Him. The more you pray healing over others, the more your faith will grow for more healing. I always see that is how faith increases.

In my experience, the reason why believers don't pray for others is because they undermine themselves. They say, "Who am I to pray? I am just a believer." All believers need to understand the Bible says you only need to be a believer to heal or to perform miracles. We all need to disciple believers to have the faith to pray for healing. A believer believes and keeps believing till it happens. Never give up if something doesn't happen right away, just keep praying and keep believing.

Bishop Michael Pfeifer: First, I encourage all people to put their total trust in Jesus and as they read the Bible, to listen closely to the Word of God and first apply this message to themselves. We need to let ourselves be healed by that loving Word, by the merciful hand of the Lord. Then those that are trying to live the Gospel are sent to be healers by Christ, to bring His healing presence to others as they let themselves be guided by the Holy Spirit. In chapter ten of Matthew's Gospel we hear about the healing mission given to the twelve—and we can say to us. "Then he summoned his twelve disciples and gave them authority over unclean spirits to drive them out and to cure every disease and every illness. . . . As you go make this proclamation: 'The kingdom of heaven is at hand.' Cure the sick, raise the dead, cleanse lepers, drive out demons.' . . . 'What I say to you in the darkness, speak in the light; and what you hear whispered, proclaim on the housetops. Whoever receives you receives me, and whoever receives me receives the one who sent me.'" (NABRE)

Pastor Jim Westheim: Let Christ be the healer and stop trying to heal them yourself. Pray, believe, and expect—and leave the outcome to God.

Mr. Worldwide Evangelist: Act like Jesus because He's in you and because He has chosen you. He's chosen believers to be His representatives and His ambassadors on the earth. He sat down at the right hand of the Father because there was nothing left for Him to do. All authority and dominion had been given to Him, and then He gave us all the keys of the kingdom. So, act like you are that beautiful ambassador, representation of Jesus Himself. He is not physically on the scene, so He sent you to physically be on the scene. So, talk with authority and dominion, and command the sickness, disease, and pain to go. Command the mental disorders to go. Command the evil spirit to leave them, breaking the power of the devil. Command healing and wholeness, and for the sickness never to return. You are releasing healing over them when you pray and lay hands on them. That's one of the ways that we are connection points with God's power. But know the moment you speak and issue that command, know your words carry power. Know John 14:12: "Very truly I tell you, whoever believes in me will do the works I have been doing, and they will do even greater things than these, because I am going to the Father." This is for you, because of the works that He did and will do now and in the future through you.

Since Jesus has given you the Holy Spirit, expect that Spirit of Power, the precious Holy Spirit, to deliver. So, anything He tells you to do as you're ministering, do it with boldness. If He says, "Move their arm gently around," then do it. If the Holy Spirit says to have them bend over, tell them to and help them to do that. Help them act their faith right then and there. And if He reveals anything more to do, follow that leading. Follow that impression. I think sometimes people stop halfway instead of fully carrying out the impressions of God of what to do, and God will see you all the way through.

Pastor Waseem Yousaf: Have a passion to believe in and perform healing miracles. I would like to encourage all believers to be obedient to our Lord's commands and faithfully serve him. If we follow Him faithfully, we can become His good disciples. When we become good disciples, we can get the blessing of healings from the Lord. Moreover, prayer and fasting are the essential parts of healing miracles. The more we pray and fast and get closer to Jesus, the more we are anointed for healing miracles. If we do not immediately see miracles, we must not quit. We must have a persistent attitude when we pray for healings. So, we need practice for healing in prayers and intercession for people.

Chapter 24

WHAT ARE SOME REAL HEALING STORIES?

There are many great healing stories in the Bible, and throughout this book we have looked at a number of these stories in addition to examples of amazing modern healings witnessed by me and those interviewed for this book. In this section, you will see a mix of real healing stories from our ministry leaders. In some stories people were healed miraculously, and in some they were not healed here on earth. I felt it was important to show both sides, as it represents the reality of healing today.

> **Apostle Les Bowling**: I vividly remember a story from when I was young, around seven years old. I was a bad boy—well, as bad as a seven-year-old could be—and I was not born again. One night I was sick to my stomach. My mom was a believer, and I'll never forget what she said: "Son, I'm going to pray for you to be healed, and the Lord is going to heal you." When she prayed for me, I felt like a heavy weight, which had been over my body, lifted from me, and I didn't feel sick. I have never forgotten that, even to this day, and I knew the God that she was always talking about was real. I didn't want to be a "bad boy" after that happened.
>
> Here is a true story from a pastor I personally know from Latvia, one of the Baltic nations under the former Soviet Union. He was in a bad car wreck, resulting in a break in his spine, and he became paralyzed. The doctors told him there was no hope for recovery, and this would

be his lot for the rest of his life. As a pastor, he was a strong believer. He said somebody gave him an old Oral Roberts VCR tape on healing. It had been played so much there wasn't even an image, but you could still hear it. He listened to that tape for two days straight, playing it repeatedly. He clung to Oral Roberts's words: "Not only did Christ pay the price for your sins, he paid the price for your healing. And if God's put a calling and purpose on your life, he wants you to be healed to fulfill that call." The pastor meditated on that for two days. Then, supernaturally he got up and walked right out of that hospital. He had never understood before that Christ had already paid the price for his healing. Once he heard and believed, he was healed.

Director Jill Boyonas: My favorite healing story happened on the island of Mindanao in the Philippines. I don't have the Holy Spirit Gifts of Healing, but whenever I go to new areas, God will sometimes use healings, signs, wonders, and miracles to open the doors for our ministry in that area. The local bishops in this area did not believe in healings or miracles, but they were interested to learn more about it. So, we held a Bible service for them, and even though the crowd was small, the presence of the Lord was really strong. Then, in walked the seventy-five-year-old widow of a previous bishop, and her name was Lola. She was very sick, could barely walk, and was ready to go be with her dead husband, but she let me pray for her. When I laid my hands on her, she was slain in the Spirit and gently fell to the floor. The problem is she was sleeping in the Spirit, and she lay on the floor for over an hour until almost everyone was gone from the meeting. I woke her up, and she went home. She returned early the next day with amazing news. She said, "Last night God healed me. In fact, I feel like I'm sixteen years old, and I want to go with you on your mission trip." That day she walked with us for seven miles in the mountain without problem and was even the first one to get to our destination.

Pastor Lisa Chin: I suffered from both eczema and anemia when I was younger. Though I endured both for an extended period, in both instances the Lord healed me, just when I needed it the most. I still do have some eczema problems but it is not as bad as it was before.

I have also had friends, church members, and family members not receive healing or pain relief for their illnesses. Sadly, I had a friend who refused to take any medication, even though she had diabetes. She was hoping to be healed, but she died. It could have been managed with medication.

Missionary Jared Dietrich: This is a salvation and healing story. The predominant religion and worldview in Mongolia is Tibetan Buddhism mixed with Shamanism, which is a form of animism where people believe there are spirits in many different things. The Shaman is a person the Mongolian people believe have special abilities to communicate with these spirits and even compel them to do his or her will. When people go to the Shaman with a need, they must pay the Shaman money to pray for them to influence the spirits in their favor.

Once time, a high school student named Teresa (alias) was coming to our English-speaking club and Bible study group. She was curious but had not yet made any decision to follow Jesus. Then one day, she told our group she was worried about her grandmother who was very sick. Her Grandma was in a faraway village but was unable to travel because of her failing health. We told Teresa that Jesus is a healing God and that we would be happy to take her to visit her grandmother's home and pray for her.

My wife, Boggie, and I took Teresa to visit her grandmother at her parent's home. Her grandmother was staying alone in a separate ger, or a round Mongolian hut, so she wouldn't be exposed to a lot of family members and get sicker. So just Boggie and Teresa went to meet with her grandmother.

When Boggie and Teresa went into the ger, this sweet grandma was in her bed. She seemed very tired and weak but made an effort to sit up and greet Boggie. They chatted for a while and then Boggie began sharing the Gospel story with this grandma. Boggie told her all Jesus had done for her and how she could also receive this Jesus into her heart. The Holy Spirit was very present in that ger and Grandma hung on every word as Boggie spoke. After sharing for a while, Boggie asked her if she would like to pray together to receive Jesus into her heart. Grandma had a look that she wanted to say yes but had a hesitation. She told Boggie she would have to ask her kids first before she could do something like that. Boggie felt a check in her spirit and felt she should ask more about that. Boggie found out that Grandma's hesitation was her thought that Boggie was like a typical Shaman and would expect to be paid a large sum to pray for her. Grandma had little money, and she worried about a debt her children would be forced to pay. Boggie smiled and said, "Grandma, unlike other gods and spirits, what my God Jesus has to offer is completely free. *It has been paid in full.* You don't have to ask anyone or give me anything. All you need to do is believe." "Really?" Grandma asked, very surprised, "Then yes, I want to receive Jesus!" The three of them prayed together and Grandma was saved that day.

The next day, Teresa called us very excited that her grandma got up that morning completely healed! She had her strength, had gotten out of bed, and was making plans to travel and visit her home village. Teresa said, "I have seen with my own eyes, and I can't deny that Jesus is real. I want to be a Christian too!"

My most difficult story was my own mother dying from lung cancer when she was sixty. We prayed and many people prayed, but she passed away. I don't know why she passed, but God does. I will not stop praying for and believing for healing.

Pastor Naomi Dowdy: Well, I just turned ninety years old, and I'm still going strong in my ministry and traveling around the world teaching and training up pastors and leaders. The Lord has kept me strong and of sound mind to do His work. My goal now is to baptize a new believer on my hundredth birthday.

I have a missionary associate who had an interesting healing situation in his life. He and his wife were traveling missionaries and evangelists based in Central America. For many years they went to Costa Rica and other Latin American countries to do open-air crusades to preach and teach on healing. Then suddenly, he woke up one morning totally paralyzed and could not get out of bed. His wife had to get him out of bed, bathe, and dress him. However, he did not stop any of the ministry he was doing and just kept preaching and teaching from the wheelchair. He went back to Costa Rica every year for the healing crusades, preaching healing from a wheelchair. He would tell the people, "Don't look at me, you look to God; it's God's Word, God's Word heals; this wheelchair is not who I am." He never changed his message about healing, even though he was in the wheelchair. He was in the wheelchair for over ten years, and that's when I met him. Shortly after that, I got a message from him. They went back to Costa Rica, and as he was in a wheelchair, preaching about healing, suddenly the power of God hit him. He jumped out of his wheelchair, and he was running all over the place, totally healed.

Apostle Lana Heightley: My very favorite healing story is my story. I could not have children after five years of marriage. The doctors told me my ovaries were not developed and were like a small child's, and I would never conceive. I was barren. One day my sister called me, shortly after adopting a baby boy. She said, "Don't you want your own child as well?" I explained what the doctors told me about my condition. She said, "Well, that's baloney. We're going to fast and pray." So, we did for three days in the month of November 1966. Then next month I got pregnant, and nine months later, I delivered my son Rex. Like Hannah from I Samuel 1, I dedicated Rex to the Lord, and he now serves as pastor for a home church, along with working as an executive vice president for a big international company.

I have a very difficult story about my mom. Right after my mom turned fifty-one, she found out she had cervical cancer. We were all happy the surgery went well, but then six weeks later, as she was walking in the hallway of our home, her eyes crossed, and she fell. We took her back to the hospital, and they discovered she had a brain tumor. The whole family started fasting and praying for her healing, and I was believing for my mom's healing. Sadly, just a short time later she died in the hospital. I was only nineteen years old, so it was a very difficult time for me.

Superintendent Aaron Hlavin: This is more of a spiritual healing story: My mother-in-law was sick with cancer, but she was not serving the Lord. One day, my five-year-old daughter at the time, Kayla, walked into her bedroom and said, "Grandma, I know you're sick, but every kid needs a grandma in church with them." Without Kayla ever knowing, we had been trying to get my mother-in-law back into a right relationship with Jesus. And because of Kalya coming to her in such an innocent and sincere way, my mother-in-law recommitted her life to Christ. She later told us on her deathbed, "Please tell Kayla when she gets older and is having a rough time how God used her to be the greatest witness to bring her grandma back to Jesus and to die a believer." Now, seven years go by, and Kayla is twelve and going through a challenging stretch. She came to me and said, "Why won't God speak to me or speak through me?" Then I told her the whole story about her grandma. It ended up being one of the most powerful times with my daughter I've ever had in life, and gave her just what she needed at that time in her life.

Pastor Walt Landers: God did a miracle healing in our family. Not long after my three kids were born, my wife, JoAnn, was impressed in her spirit to read every book she could on healing. For six months she just soaked in God's Word for healing. Then, our six-year-old daughter Erica was diagnosed with cancer. When that happened, JoAnn turned into "superwoman" with things concerning Erica's care. Even though it was metastatic stage IV cancer, JoAnn had her finger on those doctors every step of the way. We believed and declared that Erica would be healed, and we spoke that every step of the way, in every doctor's appointment and hospital visit. It wasn't an easy road, but God healed Erica. Now, she is in her thirties, with a master's in special education, and making a huge impact. She's making a difference on other kids and students and in her world. God's Word was true.

I was a part of the healing story for this author, Merrily Madero. She was attending the church I pastor in San Angelo, TX, when she received her pancreatic cancer diagnosis. We were just coming out of Erica's cancer situation. I remember we prayed for her in faith at the church before she departed for the Whipple surgery in San Antonio. We sent two of her friends to be with her, right before and after her surgery. I also remember several of us traveling to San Antonio and praying over her after her surgery. Merrily was well known and loved at the church, and a huge number of the church rose up to pray over her. It was like those friends of the crippled man who tore through the roof to lower the crippled man down to be near Jesus so He would pray for him (Luke 5:17-19). My church in San Angelo really covered Merrily in prayer, and she was healed.

Pastor Powell Lemons: In my personal experience as a pastor, virtually every single time I've had a word of knowledge about someone having a specific pain or issue, and I have prayed for them, they have been healed. That is how the Lord works through me. Here are two examples:

One Sunday at church, during altar ministry prayer time, I sensed someone was having bad itching, burning, and stinging. I received this word of knowledge and felt led to walk over to a specific woman, and I just said to her, "This itching, burning, and stinging, I command you to leave this body in the name of Jesus Christ." Then I went out, and I didn't think about it again. The following Wednesday night, the same woman came straight over to me. She said, "You prayed for me Sunday, and I had shingles from the tops of my feet to my waist, and I was miserable. Now it is all gone, except for a tiny spot on my ankle." The Lord gave me a word of knowledge, I prayed, and she was healed.

During another Sunday service, I was singing and lost in worship when I saw a vivid picture in my mind. I saw a woman driving a car up to a busy intersection, and her car was T-boned, and then she was in a great deal of pain. So, I walked up to the pulpit after worship, and I said, "I think the Lord has spoken to me here this morning. Somebody here has been in an auto accident this past week. You were T-boned by another car, on your right or left shoulder, and they're very, very sore today, and the Lord wants to heal you." No one said anything, so I continued with the service. However, later that afternoon, I got a call from "Lorraine," who said, "Pastor, that was me. I don't know why I didn't raise my hand when you asked who needed prayer. But right after you said that, my shoulder was completely healed."

When I was in high school, I had the faith to heal myself. I tore a cartilage playing football, and my knee swelled up like a big watermelon. The doctor said they would need to do surgery the following week. On Sunday morning, at church, I was the first to have a prayer request. I remember standing in the church praying for healing and feeling the "heat of the Lord" come into my body and heal my knee. The next week the doctors were amazed my knee was healed without surgery. I continued to play football and was the all-star center for Los Angeles County.

Reverend Merrily Madero: Sometimes the answer to prayer isn't healing but hope and a plan for the future. One night my husband and I were at the Flying W Ranch in Colorado, attending dinner and a show. I started a good conversation with the woman sitting next to me from another state, who was there with her husband, who was in a wheelchair. She told me her husband had been active in sports and coaching all his life; then over the course of just a few months, he lost all feeling and use in his legs. No doctor could explain why. She told me he really struggled with why God would let this happen to him and didn't even want to attend church anymore. For the last year, he had planned this huge road trip, visiting places all over the USA that were handicap accessible. The next day they were going home from their extended road trip, and she was worried he would get depressed again with no purpose in his life. She asked if I would pray for her husband for healing. Sometimes when I pray for people, the Holy Spirit will give me a vision for them. As I was praying for this man, I saw a vision of him in his wheelchair, leading a group of young people also in wheelchairs. He was teaching them and guiding them on how to cope with life in a wheelchair. As I explained the vision, both the man and his wife got so emotional and were very grateful. I exchanged several texts with the woman over the following months, and she said her husband had a new lease on life and was excited the Lord had called him to be a blessing to others with similar struggles he faced. He received hope and a vision of a new future.

Sadly, one time I was asked to pray for a middle-aged woman who had a lingering illness. I could sense a spirit of sickness on her, but she was not willing to let go of it. She was wrapped up in the identity of her sickness and kept saying, "I'm just this way; my mom had it, and my grandma had it." Her sickness was tied to her identity, and her lifestyle. I sensed she was content to have her husband and other family members constantly wait on her and wasn't willing to let go of that sickness. We know Jesus came to reverse those conditions, but someone is not going to receive healing unless they believe it and let go of that spirit of sickness.

Missionary Mary: One night we were doing local ministry, and there were four paralyzed, middle-aged men seated in chairs at the far back of the village basketball court. So, I went to them and asked if I could pray for them. And the spirit of faith came upon me, and I knew in my spirit, "This is easy; paralysis is no big deal." Which was really the Holy

Spirit Gift of Faith. The first three men all had had strokes, so they had some paralysis on one side of their body, and as I prayed, they were all healed instantly. They were all moving and testing out their newly found mobility. The last guy was different though. He had been thrown from a horse and was paralyzed from the neck down, and his friends had to carry him anytime he wanted to go somewhere. It had been years since his accident, so the muscles on his legs had shrunk since he never used them. Thankfully, he had faith to be healed, and I had faith to pray for him. So, we prayed together, and I took hold of his legs, and I could physically feel muscles growing in his legs. Then, he had the urge and wanted to stand up, and he did. By then, the ministry program was closing, and the team was passing out little booklets to get a free Bible. The healed man said, "I want to get my own." So, he walked across the basketball court to the stage to get his own book, with his friends helping him walk for the first time in years.

One night, a boy who had been living with a severe mental illness, who was mostly non-verbal came to our meeting. We prayed for him, and he was healed. But the fun part was the following day, he was the first to arrive for our Bible study, and he was just talking, talking, talking. Then, he was telling everybody in the village what had happened to him. He was yelling out, "Hey, everybody, this really works. Get over here and have your brain healed."

My favorite deliverance story was really peaceful, once we figured out what the problem was. During an evening outreach, we prayed for a young girl who was demon-possessed and manifesting and crying out, but nothing happened. When I heard about this family's situation, I asked their pastor to bring me to their home. There were probably about a dozen adults sitting outside and at least that many kids playing around, and they were all the same family. We gathered the family to talk before I went to see the girl. The pastor had been ministering to the entire family in the past, but they also kept going back to the witch doctor whenever one of them had sickness or problems. We explained they cannot keep dabbling in witchcraft and then expect God to bless their household. So, they all agreed to stop seeing the witch doctor and they all wanted to follow Jesus whole-heartedly. After praying with the adults, we went inside the house. The girl had been convulsing and manifesting the entire time we were there. I first noticed she had on a huge religious necklace; when we asked her mother to remove it, she immediately calmed down. Her mom told me she hadn't talked for months, so we started to pray. We noticed other items on her, like bracelets that were witchcraft-related items. She had items sewn into her clothes that were also witchcraft symbols. She was covered head to toe with amulets, and other trinkets. As her mom started to remove them, the girl received more and more healing. It was the most peaceful deliverance I've ever experienced. Once everything had been removed, we said to the devil, "You do not have a place here anymore, and you must go." And it was like an evil presence was sucked out the window. The girl immediately sat up and started talking. She looked at her family and said, "I am okay now." We all gave glory to God for saving and filling this family with his presence.

Here is a hard story to tell: We headed out to do outreach in a remote tribal area. As soon as we arrived, we met a young couple who had a very sick baby, who was coughing and having trouble breathing. We prayed for the baby and the couple and sent them to a town with a hospital a couple hours' walk away. The couple returned a short time later because the baby had died. We were left alone in a small hut with the baby's body, so I thought, *We will pray for the baby to come back to life*. We prayed, but the baby did not come back to life. That one was heart breaking.

Pastor David Paul: My favorite story would be of my precious wife, Ruby. She had really bad scoliosis of her spine, and it was really curved. In 2014, doctors said that it would take at least two years for her to recover with a brace. With prayer and deliverance, she recovered within two months, and her spine became totally straight. Even today, it amazes me to review the before-and-after X-rays.

Many years ago, I was allowed into the intensive care unit (ICU) to pray for a man who was fighting with death. They normally don't let anyone go into the ICU when someone is in that bad of condition. He had taken a huge dose of poison and was trying to kill himself. I did not even know what to say, but I just prayed as the Lord led me. Then, the very next day he was returned to normal, and all the poison was gone.

Sadly, we lost a dear member of our congregation a short time ago, and she was only forty-five years old. She had cancer in her feet. It was diagnosed early, but she didn't tell us about it until they had to amputate her left leg at the knee to stop the spread. Even then, the whole church believed for healing, and we pooled our money to get her a high-quality artificial leg. Through our faith, we believed to see her walking, healed and whole. However, after the amputation, her health declined faster than ever, and she left us quickly. It was hard for the church to see her go, but everyone was happy to know she was with Jesus in heaven.

Mr. Worldwide Evangelist: We have seen thousands of healings at our crusades around the world. But, my all-time favorite story of healing is the story of "N" and her niece. N was a Buddhist Thai lady, and her niece was dying of full-blown AIDS at six years old. N carried her to one of our crusades, because the niece had stopped eating altogether. N had to mush up all her food because she had stopped eating all solids, and she was very dehydrated. N said, "Lord Jesus, if you are real, heal my niece, and I'll give my life to serve you." God did His work, and He touched that niece and healed her. But that miracle dominoed in so many ways, as the whole family came to know Jesus. We've tracked N and her niece, who is now in college studying the Word of God and wants to operate cross-culturally and among different language groups. All because of an amazing story of the healing power of God.

My toughest healing story was myself. When you are so used to flowing in healing for others, and you're used to living in kind of a state of divine life and health, self-healing can be difficult. For me it was just a simple planter wart on my heel. I went to a doctor, who cut it out, but he reminded me they can come back if they don't get all the roots. Well, I took all the precautions of letting it heal up properly. But a short time later, I noticed it had come back, and I got angry about it. So, I took my knife, and I tried to cut it out myself, to save several hundred dollars to have another procedure done. Well, then it came back with a vengeance, doubled in size, and I began to get bombarded with thoughts of fear. Thoughts like, *You turned this into some weird cell pattern growth; it's a cancer now.* All these terrible thoughts were hitting me, no doubt from the enemy. So, I just began to quote the Word, but all the while I was saying those things, it was still growing larger. But I just kept thanking God for His healing. At first there was no reaction in the right direction. But the more I just kept standing on and focusing on God's

Word, the more I became persuaded that I would be healed. One day I was cleaning it, and it had no longer grown bigger. It began to retract and was beginning to shrink. I said, "See, that's the truth, devil. You're defeated. You're under my feet. This thing is shrinking. It's dying at the roots. It's withering at the cellular level." Soon it was completely gone, with no trace of even the scars from the two cuts. Don't let the enemy dupe you. Stand on the Word. It's eternal.

Pastor Jim Westheim: I would like to share a difficult healing story. I grieved when I lost my parents, but my dad was eighty-seven and my mom was ninety, so they both lived strong, healthy lives. The toughest sickness and death I had to endure was Karen Hlavin, wife of our Michigan Network Superintendent at the time, Jeff Hlavin. Karen had a very special kindness within her, and she had a special place in my heart. She helped me through the most difficult struggles that I ever went through in my many years of ministry. She was always a willing ear to listen, and knew exactly what to say or not say. I would call the Hlavin house, and if Jeff answered, I'd say "Jeff, can I talk to your wife?" and he knew what that was about. She really helped me stay on track in my thinking and in some areas that were really a challenge for me.

Then Karen got sick and went downhill very quickly. I labored with God that it was not right that she got so sick, so quickly. I started praying for her, more than she was praying for me. Her sickness absolutely eclipsed her. I cried out, "This is not right. She's too young for this to happen." But I had to let go of that. I began realizing that God was doing something far greater, and I had to let go of my insisting that God heal her and let God be God. I've watched how Jeff has worked with her loss, and it's been a wonderful journey God has used in that direction. I miss her tremendously, but I recognize that healing wasn't for her at that point in the way that we wanted it to happen. God brought it about in a much better way for Karen.

Chapter 25
WHAT ARE SOME SAMPLE HEALING PRAYERS?

Basic Healing Prayer

Thank You, Father, for loving me.
I praise You for the mighty God You are.
I know I am a sinner and confess my sins to You.
Please forgive me of my sins.
In Jesus' name, heal me.
In line with Your will, heal me either miraculously, medically, progressively, or eternally.
I bind any demonic influence and say, "You must flee in the name of Jesus."
I have the faith to believe I'm healed.
Lord, heal this area of my body: _____.
I will walk out in faith, believing I am healed.
In Jesus' name I pray, amen.

Healing Prayer for the Spirit

Father God, I praise Your holy name.
I ask for healing in my spirit, as my spirit is not aligned with Your Holy Spirit.
I confess my sins to You and ask for Your forgiveness.
I bind any demonic spiritual influence and say, "You must flee in the name of Jesus Christ."
Open my ears to hear clearly from Your Holy Spirit.

Bring my spirit back into relationship with the Holy Spirit.
I surrender my will to Your will and ask You to guide my steps.
Thank You, Father, for healing my spirit and guiding my steps as I walk in Your will and in Your ways.
In Jesus' name I pray, amen.

Healing Prayer for the Soul

Father God, I give You praise and glory.
I ask for healing in my soul, as my mind, will, and emotions are out of alignment with Your perfect will for my life.
I confess my sins to You and ask for Your forgiveness.
Open my ears to hear clearly from Your Holy Spirit.
I surrender my will to Your will and ask You to guide my steps.
I specifically need healing for this area: _____.
I declare any soul issue brought by Satan must go in the name of Jesus Christ.
Thank You, Father, for healing my soul and guiding my steps as I walk in Your will and in Your ways.
In Jesus' name I pray, amen.

Emotional Healing Prayer

Heavenly Father, I praise You and I need You.
I confess my sins to You and ask for Your forgiveness.
I need healing and peace from the many emotions I'm feeling.
I bind Satan in my thoughts and demand he leave in the name of Jesus.
Lord, I ask for these specific requests:
- Safe places to name and experience the fullness of my painful emotions.
- Quiet presence of special people to sit with me in the pain and suffering.
- Openness to receive companionship and service from others.
- Deep love and comfort from the companionship and service given by others.
- Self-care and compassion through sleep, hydration, nutrition, and movement.

Please guide me if I am to seek professional help.
Thank You, Father, for healing my emotions and guiding my steps as I walk in Your will and in Your ways.
In Jesus' name I pray, amen.

Physical Healing Prayer

Holy Father, I give You all my praise and worship.
I confess my sins to You and ask for Your forgiveness for those sins which may have brought about my condition.
I need healing in these areas in my body: ____.
I pray for pain relief and wisdom regarding prescriptions and over-the counter medications.
I pray for all doctors, nurses, and technicians assigned to my care—give them wisdom and discernment.
I pray over any medical procedures that are needed.
I come against any demonic presence and demand the enemy flee in the name of Jesus.
I declare any physical ailment must go in the name of Jesus Christ.
Thank You, Father, for healing my body and guiding my steps as I walk in Your will and in Your ways.
In Jesus' name I pray, amen.

End-of-Life Prayer

Father God, holy, holy, holy is Your name.
We lift up _____.
If this person doesn't know You, we pray for the opportunity to tell them about You one more time.
We pray for them to be healed either miraculously, medically, progressively, or eternally.
We pray for Your perfect will in this situation.
We pray for relief from any pain or nausea and to make them comfortable.
We pray for clarity of mind to recognize and reminisce with their family members that are here.
We pray for only positive words to be spoken during this time.
We pray for this person's desires, and Your will over their life.
We release them to You.
In Jesus' name we pray, amen.

Prayer to Heal Ourselves

Heavenly Father, I praise Your holy name.

Please forgive all my sins, especially any sins that may have contributed to this sickness or injury or troubled emotions.

Guide my steps if I need to make amends to others I may have hurt or offended.

I pray for healing in the name of Jesus.

I believe in faith for Your healing, in accordance with Your will.

In Jesus' name I pray, amen.

Prayer to Heal Our Pets

Heavenly Father, we praise You for the incredible God You are.

Your Word says to care for our pets (Proverbs 12:10), and my pet_____ needs your help.

I pray for healing for my pet.

I pray You take away their pain, discomfort, and any other issues.

Please guide me and medical professionals to care for my pet.

Make it clear to me if the best option is euthanasia so they can be with You. Then I believe I will see them when I get to heaven.

Thank You, Lord, that You care for our animals, just like we do.

In Jesus' name I pray, amen.

Appendix

STEPS TO BECOME A BELIEVER AND LEAD OTHERS TO JESUS

(Disclaimer: Some of this information I've had for decades and cannot confirm if I received it from any previous ministry organizations I worked with.)

These steps will walk you through the processes to both become a believer and to lead others to salvation and a relationship with Jesus Christ.

I. To Become a Believer
A. Read Through These "Road to Salvation" Verses
1. **Romans 3:23:** "For all have sinned and fall short of the glory of God."
2. **Romans 6:23:** "For the wages of sin is death, but the gift of God is eternal life in Christ Jesus our Lord."
3. **John 3:3:** "Jesus replied, 'Very truly I tell you, no one can see the kingdom of God unless they are born again.'"
4. **Romans 5:8:** "But God demonstrates his own love for us in this: While we were still sinners, Christ died for us."
5. **John 14:6:** "Jesus answered, 'I am the way and the truth and the life. No one comes to the Father except through me.'"
6. **Romans 10:9-10:** "If you declare with your mouth, 'Jesus is Lord,' and believe in your heart that God raised him from the dead, you will be saved. For it is with your heart that you believe and are justified, and it is with your mouth that you profess your faith and are saved."

7. **Romans 10:13:** "Everyone who calls on the name of the Lord will be saved."
8. **2 Corinthians 5:15:** "And he died for all, that those who live should no longer live for themselves but for him who died for them and was raised again."
9. **Revelation 3:20:** "Here I am! I stand at the door and knock. If anyone hears my voice and opens the door, I will come in and eat with that person, and they with me."

B. **Believe and Confess Out Loud This Gospel of Jesus Christ**
 1. Jesus was born of a virgin.
 2. Jesus showed His Father God's love while on earth.
 3. Jesus died a sinless man, on the cross, as a sacrifice for our sins.
 4. Jesus rose from the dead on the third day.
 5. Jesus walked on the earth for forty days before ascending back into heaven.
 6. Jesus will come again.

C. **Pray This Salvation Prayer Out Loud**
- Thank You, Father, for loving me.
- I know You are a mighty God, but You also care about me.
- I know I am a sinner, and I confess my sins to You.
- I believe Jesus died on the cross for my sins.
- I believe Jesus rose from the dead to ensure I will be able to spend eternity in heaven with Him.
- I surrender my will and my life to Jesus.
- In Jesus' name, heal my spirit, soul, and body.
- I will walk out in faith believing I am healed and following Your will and Your ways.

Thank You, Lord, amen.

D. **Find a Bible-Based Church and Join That Fellowship of Believers**

E. **Become Water Baptized**

Baptism in water is a symbolic act of being joined with Christ in His death, burial, and resurrection.

F. Receive the Holy Spirit
The Holy Spirit's indwelling and renewing work is part of the salvation process.

2. Questions to Ask Nonbelievers to Get Them into a Discussion About Their Faith
- Do you have any spiritual beliefs?
- Who is Jesus to you?
- Do you think there is a heaven and a hell?
- If you died today, where would you go?
- If there was a chance that what you believed was not true, what would you want to know?

3. Steps to Lead Someone to Become a Believer
a. Befriend them.
b. Share your testimony of how you came to know and follow Jesus.
c. Share the Gospel.
   - Jesus was born of a virgin.
   - Jesus showed His Father God's love while on earth.
   - Jesus died a sinless man, on the cross, as a sacrifice for our sins.
   - Jesus rose from the dead on the third day.
   - Jesus walked on the earth for forty days before ascending back into heaven.
   - Jesus will come again.

d. Ask them to make the decision to follow Jesus Christ.
e. Have them repeat out loud the prayer of salvation.
f. Either disciple them to grow in their faith or pass them off to someone else who will disciple them.

ENDNOTES

Chapter 7
1. Ed Melick, *Healing Plunge: An In-Depth Analysis of Healing in the Bible* (Grace Machines, 2019), page 10.

Chapter 8
1. Brenda Rogers is a licensed professional counselor. Her website is www.discovertruthcounseling.com and her email is Brenda@discovertruthcounceling.com.

Chapter 9
1. Brenda Rogers is a licensed professional counselor. Her website is www.discovertruthcounseling.com and her email is Brenda@discovertruthcounceling.com.

Chapter 10
1. Divine Healing | Assemblies of God (USA). Position Paper on Divine Healing. (Adopted by the General Presbytery in session August 9-11, 2010). From its inception the General Council of the Assemblies.

Chapter 11
1. Christianty.com. Https://share.google/wGtk4v9lMSFlXjl4s
2. *Oxford English Dictionary*, "bitterness," accessed September 5, 2025, https://www.oed.com/search/dictionary/?scope=Entries&q=bitterness.
3. https://biblehub.com/study/ephesians/4-31.htm#:~:text=Bitterness%20refers%20to%20a%20deep-seated%20resentment%20that,which%20can%20cause%20trouble%20and%20defile%20many.
4. *Oxford English Dictionary*, "unbelief," accessed September 5, 2025, https://www.oed.com/search/dictionary/?scope=Entries&q=unbelief.
5. Belief or Unbelief, by Bert Cargill, May 13, 2019, https://share.google/UdAeSmaMn2dTybmta

Chapter 15
1. 100 Quotes from Billy Graham www.billygraham.ca https://share.google/9n3l7tTMBukUsyQFl

Chapter 17
1. Ed Melick, *Healing Plunge: An In-Depth Analysis of Healing in the Bible* (Grace Machines, 2019), page 47.
2. David Diga Hernandez, "How Demons Enter: 4 Gateways Demons Exploit to Invade and Hijack Your Life," lookuponme, July 14, 2025, https://lookuponme.wordpress.com/2025/07/14/how-demons-enter-4-gateways-demons-exploit-to-invade-hijack-your-life/.

Chapter 18
1. Ed Melick, *Healing Plunge: An In-Depth Analysis of Healing in the Bible* (Grace Machines, 2019), page 10.

ABOUT THE AUTHOR

Merrily Madero was miraculously healed of pancreatic cancer in 2008, and now has a passion for learning as much as possible about God's healing power and spreading that knowledge to others.

Merrily is the founder and president of Merrily Madero Ministries, M3 International, and an ordained minister through Michigan Ministry Network, Assemblies of God. Through her ministry, she is called to preach, teach, and serve around the world. To date she's traveled to 119 countries and conducted ministry in twenty-four of them. She provides leadership development and management training to churches and organizations around the world, in places that need it the most. Her leadership expertise comes from serving in the U.S. Air Force for thirty years, commanding and leading airmen, soldiers, sailors, and civilians throughout her distinguished career, retiring at the rank of colonel. Merrily has bachelor degrees in both Mechanical Engineering and Theology, and advanced degrees from Troy University, Air Command and Staff College, and National Defense University.

Merrily is also the author of the book *The Truth About Consequences*, which is also available in Urdu, the primary language of Pakistan. She coauthored the book *Kingdom Chronicles: Tales of Guts, Glory, and Spiritual Authority*. Her books are available through her website (www.M3international.org) or on Amazon.

Merrily has one daughter, Dr. Leia Fecteau, MD, who is currently chief resident for the Emergency Medicine and Internal Medicine Combined Program through Northwell Health, to be followed by a Critical Care Fellowship at Jewish Long Island Medical Center in New York. Merrily is happily married to Joël Casse from Québec, Canada, who has two children, Béylnda and Raphëal Casse. They split their time between Saint Helen, Michigan; Colorado Springs, Colorado; and Québec City, Canada.

To contact Merrily for preaching, speaking, or training:

MerrilyMadero@gmail.com
M3 International
PO Box 76322
Colorado Springs, CO 80907-6322,
USA

Be sure to check out her website: www.M3international.org.